Top Tips and Traps

TIP

Buy the right house, in the right neighborhood, at the right price, and no matter how bad the market may get, you'll always sell for good value. (Chapter 1)

TIP

A "buyer's market" doesn't necessarily mean it's a good time to buy. It may mean that savvy buyers are staying out of the market. (Chapter 2)

TIP

There are no price restrictions, only mortgage restrictions. Don't think, "How high a price can I afford?" Think, "How big a mortgage can I get?" (Chapter 5)

TIP

Sellers are often hung up on price. Offer them their full price and they may give you ridiculously favorable terms. (Chapter 9)

TRAP

Adjustable-rate mortgages, in general and for many people, are traps. They contain numerous pitfalls that the average borrower just isn't aware of. (Chapter 5)

TRAP

Don't shop for a home by car. Nothing substitutes for "walking the block" when it comes to discovering the kind of neighborhood you're in. (Chapter 6)

TIP

You'll pay more for a pool house, and probably enjoy it less. A fireplace and air conditioning are considered standard these days, so you should pay less for a house that doesn't have them. (Chapter 6)

TRAP

Don't let your agent discourage you from offering a low price. Remember, your agent gets a commission when the deal closes at any price. You only get a good deal when you get your price. (Chapter 9)

TIP

When interest rates are low, get a fixed-rate mortgage and lock in the low rate. When interest rates are high, consider an adjustable-rate mortgage, with payments that fall as interest rates come down. (Chapter 11)

TIP

If you have a credit blemish or have trouble otherwise qualifying, shop for a lender, not an interest rate. (Chapter 11)

TRAP

Remember, if you wait until escrow is ready to close to complain, it's too late. (Chapter 12)

Tips and Traps When Buying a Home

Other McGraw-Hill Books by Robert Irwin

Tips and Traps When Selling a Home, Second Edition

Tips and Traps When Mortgage Hunting

Tips and Traps for Making Money in Real Estate

Buy, Rent, & Hold: How to Make Money in a "Cold" Real Estate Market

How to Find Hidden Real Estate Bargains, Revised First Edition

The McGraw-Hill Real Estate Handbook, Second Edition

Tips and Traps When Negotiating Real Estate

Tips and Traps When Buying a Home

Robert Irwin

Second Edition

McGraw-Hill

New York San Francisco Washington, D.C. Auckland Bogotá
Caracas Lisbon London Madrid Mexico City Milan
Montreal New Delhi San Juan Singapore
Sydney Tokyo Toronto

Library of Congress Cataloging-in-Publication Data

Irwin, Robert.
Tips and traps when buying a home / Robert Irwin. — 2nd ed.
p. cm.
Includes index.
ISBN 0-07-032884-6
1. House buying. 2. Real estate business. I. Title.
HD1379.I67 1996
643′.12—dc20 96-9176
CIP

McGraw-Hill

A Division of The ***McGraw-Hill*** *Companies*

3 4 5 6 7 8 9 0 DOC/DOC 9 0 1 0 9 8

ISBN 0-07-032884-6

The sponsoring editor for this book was David Conti, the editing supervisor was Patricia V. Amoroso, and the production supervisor was Donald F. Schmidt. It was set in Baskerville by Victoria Khavkina of McGraw-Hill's Professional Book Group composition unit.

Printed and bound by R. R. Donnelley & Sons Company.

This book contains the author's opinions. Some material in this book may be affected by changes in the law (or changes in interpretations of the law) or changes in market conditions since the manuscript was prepared. Therefore, the accuracy and completeness of the information contained in this book and the opinions based on it cannot be guaranteed. Neither the author nor the publisher is engaged in rendering investment, legal, tax, accounting, or other similar professional services. If these services are required, the reader should obtain them from a competent professional. The publisher and author hereby specifically disclaim any liability for loss incurred as a consequence of following any advice or applying information presented in this book.

This book is printed on recycled, acid-free paper containing a minimum of 50% recycled, de-inked fiber.

Contents

Preface

> This year over 3 million people will buy either a new home or a resale. For many of you it will be your first home purchase. For others it will be a transaction they do less than half a dozen times in a lifespan.

When I wrote those words at the beginning of the first edition to this book several years ago, I never dreamed that they would become part of one of the best-selling real estate "how to" books, ever.

My main goal then was to thread a safe path for the home buyer through the minefield of dealing with brokers, sellers, attorneys, escrow officers, lenders, and documents that are all part of a home purchase. I knew that without a reliable guide, purchasing a home is confusing, difficult, and even frightening. I wanted this book to be that guide.

And I still do.

This new edition is completely rewritten and contains the latest information on handling home inspections, getting low-down, low-interest-rate mortgages, analyzing neighborhoods, dealing with agents, and much more to protect you in a home purchase. It is filled with answers organized to anticipate your questions. I've attempted to give you good guidelines to follow and to warn you in advance of traps that you will encounter.

I hope that this new up-to-date edition will help you, the reader, easily and confidently find and purchase the ideal home of your dreams at a price you can afford.

Robert Irwin

Tips and Traps When Buying a Home

1
New Tips on Home Buying

Has it been a while since you bought a home? Is this your first purchase?

If you've been out of the market for even a short time, or have never before purchased, be aware that the face of real estate has changed in the last few years. Buying a home today is a far different experience than it used to be.

TIP

Remember, you make your profit when you buy, not when you sell. Buy the right house, in the right neighborhood, at the right price and no matter how bad the market may get, you can always sell for good value.

Today, savvy buyers don't just look at homes or neighborhoods in general. They first look specifically at the quality of schools and the crime rate within a neighborhood. They check out homeowners' associations and watch for cosmetically "fixed" homes. And they search for the "high tech" house as well as the "golden fit."

Savvy buyers know that the rules of purchase have changed: Today detailed home inspections, long and complex purchase contracts, and innovative financing are commonly used. Even the way real estate is offered for sale has a new look with buyer's agents, discount brokers and many more FSBOs (homes for sale by owner) available.

We'll cover all these areas and many more in this book. But first, here are six quick tips to help get you up to speed.

1. Beware of High- or Even Moderate-Crime Neighborhoods

In the past, few home buyers checked out the crime statistics for a neighborhood. Most felt that if you wanted to be safe, you simply bought in the low-crime suburbs. Stay away from the inner cities and you wouldn't get hurt.

But in recent years gang and drug problems, thefts, muggings, rape, and even murder have come to the suburbs. Now, many of the outlying areas have their own crime problems.

As a result, the first questions that home buyers often ask, whether near a large urban area or in the country, has to do with personal safety. You should ask these questions, too. (Even if you aren't especially worried for yourself, buying in a low-crime area will greatly enhance your ability to resell later on.)

- How safe is the neighborhood?
- Will I feel comfortable strolling the streets after dark?
- Can my children walk to school unescorted?
- Can I leave my car unlocked in my driveway and expect it and its contents to be there the next morning?
- Do I need a home burglar alarm system?
- Do I need bars on the windows and a steel front door?

How Do You Get Answers?

Make a quick call to your local police precinct, substation, or administrative office. (Don't call 911; it's for emergencies only—call information or use the yellow pages.) Ask the desk officer for crime statistics for the city and particular neighborhood you are considering. All police departments keep these figures. They should be able to supply you with current numbers as well as comparisons with previous years (so you can see whether the crime rate is going up or down), and they should be broken down by type of crime as well as by neighborhood.

Also, consider using the "graffiti index." This is my own unofficial measurement for the level of crime in a neighborhood. It assumes that the greater the amount of graffiti on fences and store and home walls in a neighborhood, the greater the potential amount of crime. On the other hand, no graffiti at all indicates a fairly crime-free area.

Of course in today's world, it seems that "taggers," or those who tag walls with graffiti, abound everywhere. However, in low-crime areas, pride of ownership by the residents gets them out there removing and painting over the graffiti as soon as it's put up. In high-crime areas, however, people are often afraid to remove the graffiti, or have become worn down by the large amount of it, and simply let it coexist—a bad sign.

TRAP

You can always buy a house in a high-crime area for less money than one in a low-crime area. But later on it will be more difficult to resell and will bring you a lower return on your investment.

2. Look for High-Quality Neighborhood Schools

High-quality education applies *whether or not* you have school-age children.

One of the most important facts with which you can come away from this book is that what determines home values, almost more than anything else in neighborhoods, is the quality of the local schools. Please be sure you "hear" what I've written. If you're concerned about "location, location, location," check out the schools first—they will determine the true quality of your location.

Over the past 35 years in real estate, I have seen this happen time and again. Two comparable neighborhoods will start off with relatively equal types of homes and locales. But whereas one passes bond measure after bond measure to reduce class sizes, build new school site facilities, and add cultural activities to the teaching program such as music, art, and extra sports, the other never passes those bond measures. The inevitable result is that the first neighborhood produces excellent-quality schools, while the second produces much poorer ones. And over time the neighborhood with the high-quality schools sees significantly higher home price appreciation than the neighborhood with poorer-quality schools. In fact, in the latter the value of homes often stagnates or even declines.

In short, there is a direct correlation between the quality of schools and the value of homes. It's as simple as good schools mean homes go up in value; bad schools mean they don't. A smart buyer will always look to future resale. One of the best ways of ensuring you will sell for far more than you paid is to buy into a neighborhood with excellent schools.

TRAP

Don't make the mistake of comparing tax bills by neighborhood and then buying into the lower-taxed area. Low taxes mean low services (poor schools), and today's buyers want services, especially good schools. Don't be penny wise and pound foolish.

How Do You Find Good Schools?

Look for high scores on national and state tests. Check with the local school district's administrative office. High scores are in the eightieth percentile or better and indicate a good school district.

Also visit the school site that your neighborhood feeds. Check out its test scores (compared with other schools in the district). Look for clean, freshly painted facilities. Interview the principal and a few teachers (if possible) and ask if the district provides adequate books and learning materials and caters to students' individual needs. (Does it have special programs for learning-impaired as well as gifted and talented students?)

TRAP

Just because a house you are considering has a great neighborhood school, don't assume that your kids will automatically be able to go to it. Remember, a lot of other parents will be trying to get their kids into the same good school too, sometimes resulting in overcrowding. Impacted schools may refuse to accept new students. Check with the principal to see if there's a waiting list and how far away and how good the alternate school is.

3. Beware of Cosmetically "Fixed" Houses

This caveat only applies if you are buying a resale or "used" home, not a brand-new one. (There are roughly three to four times as many resales purchased each year as brand-new properties.)

Many times, particularly in older neighborhoods, investors will purchase rundown homes and then fix them up for resale. These "fixer-uppers" can be bought for much less than market price because of their poor condition, then fixed up and resold for a much higher price. If you're looking for a lower-priced, rundown home in a pricy neighborhood, you should check them out. Also read my book *Find It, Buy It, Fix It* (1996).

Problems arise, however, when the investor doesn't do the necessary work, but only covers it up cosmetically. Such a house may "show" wonderfully, but after a few years you might need a new roof, new furnace, plumbing repairs, and much, much more.

You may pay top dollar, only to discover later that you must pour in additional money to fix serious defects.

How Do You Spot a Bad Fixer?

You should always suspect any older home that has been "modernized" with a new kitchen and bath. You should also be wary of resales that have recently been repainted inside and out—new paint can hide a world of sins.

Don't rely on the seller to disclose all defects. In many states (but not all) sellers are required to disclose defects. But they may leave off something important (or may not even know a problem exists).

Hire a competent home inspector (see Chapter 13) and check it out with him or her. Pay special attention to furnaces and water heaters (anything older than 10 years is suspect), plumbing (watch out for old galvanized steel), foundations (look for cracks), and roofs (go into the attic to see if daylight is shining through). Be wary when there's new paint on foundation walls or no cracks anywhere in the house; it may just mean they've been cosmetically covered up. (All older homes have *some* cracks in them.)

TIP

Find out how long the seller has owned the property. Your agent may know, or if he doesn't, check out the county records where all sales are recorded. Be doubly wary if the present seller has owned the home only a short time—6 months or less. Your house that looks so wonderful now may have been a damaged fixer-upper only months earlier.

TRAP

Be sure that all major work was done with a building permit and has been inspected and properly approved. A quick call or a short trip to the local building department will give you the answer.

4. Look for the Energy-Efficient, High-Tech Home

Fuel costs are high and rising, making it increasingly expensive to heat and cool a house. In the future (when you want to resell) this will be an even more important consideration for buyers. Energy-efficient homes will bring a premium on the market and will sell more quickly. If you're going to spend the big money required to buy a home, you will do better to buy one that is energy-efficient and high-tech ready.

What Should You Ask and Look For?

Ask if the house is "fully" insulated, meaning insulation not only in the ceiling but in the walls and under the floors as well. Also ask to see the seller's actual bills for gas (or oil) and electric service going back 2 years. (Surprisingly, most owners keep these; if they don't, get their permission to call the gas, oil, or electric company for actual bills.) The cost will vary depending on the size of the home and the climate. Anything over $100 a month for a small condo (for gas, oil, and electric) should be considered high-end. Anything over $200 a month for a 2000-square-foot house, likewise, should be considered high-end.

TRAP

Avoid houses that are heated electrically or use inefficient gas furnaces. An efficient gas furnace is one that is rated 90 percent efficient or higher. Avoid homes with air conditioning that has an energy rating of below 12.

TIP

Look for high-efficiency gas furnaces and air conditioners by Amana and Lennox. Look for a wood-burning "pellet" stove. Check for a combination heating/cooling "heat pump." Look for a "zone system" that allows you to close off and not heat or cool designated areas of the house that aren't being used.

Also look for "high-tech ready." If you're Bill Gates (owner of Microsoft Corporation) "high-tech ready" probably means that when you enter the home, you put on a little key that alerts the house to your exact location at any given moment. That way, the house can turn lights on and off as you pass through rooms, turn on the surround sound system to your favorite music, or put your choice of TV shows on screen for you. (It can probably start your coffee and pop your toast, as well!)

Chances are that the house or condo you're considering won't be that high-tech. But you should look for at least two-phone line availability, hookups for cable TV, all outside electrical connections underground (as opposed to being in the air on telephone poles), and maybe even one of the new, small digital satellite dishes already installed.

Also, be sure the house is high-tech retrofitted (if it's a resale) to handle natural disasters. Depending on the type of natural calamity that strikes your area of the country, check to see if the home has been designed to withstand earthquakes, hurricanes, or tornadoes.

5. Be Wary of Homeowner Associations

If you are considering a condominium, townhouse, or co-op, you will have some form of homeowner association, or HOA. Even many individual homes today also require, in their deeds, that you belong to an HOA.

The idea behind HOAs is a good one. The HOA will see that everyone keeps up the front yard (or will directly take care of the front yard for you), make sure that no one alters a home to conflict with the architectural style of the area, and maintain and make available any amenities (such as pools) that are owned in common.

Problems occur because homeowner associations have a tendency to overregulate, and many times their monthly fees become excessive. The result can be trouble while you live there and trouble later on when you want to resell.

Further, few homeowners have the time or inclination to serve on the governing board of the HOA. (Will you be willing to give up two to four Saturdays a month to help run the organization?) Thus, too often only those who want political power (albeit at a low level) or have an axe to grind will run and be elected. And often their regulatory and financial decisions are capricious.

How Do You Determine If an HOA Is Good or Bad?

As a prospective buyer, you should examine the records of the HOA. Check out the number of lawsuits filed against it in the previous 5 years. A well-run HOA will have none or at most one. A poorly run HOA will have multiple lawsuits, some of which may still be pending and which could adversely affect your ability to arrange financing. Naturally, it will be more difficult to resell your home in an HOA that has lots of lawsuits against it.

Also, look at the current and past record of dues going back to the beginning of the organization. A well-run HOA will have a history of very gradual dues increases (increased to cover inflation). A poorly run HOA will have initially low dues followed by sudden and very high increases.

TRAP

Be prepared to pay high HOA dues. These are in addition to your normal taxes, mortgage, insurance, and utilities payments. Today, dues of between $125 to $300 per month are not in any way uncommon.

6. Look for a Home That Has the "Golden Fit"

Too many buyers look for homes with their eyes and not their minds. It's too easy to be enamored with a Cape Cod façade in front, or a cute little fireplace in the master bedroom, or an adorable cutting-block counter in the kitchen. What you should be looking for is a home that fits your specific needs. Of course, that means that you'll have to spend a little time defining what those needs are. When you have, however, and the home matches, it's a "golden fit." This doesn't mean that you can't fall in love with a home. What I'm talking about is the difference between a short infatuation and a long-term relationship.

Today, as never before, a house has to do quadruple duty as an office, a recreation area, an entertainment center, a storage facility—and even more. Here are some typical needs and the home design that makes them golden fits.

What You Have	*What You Need*
Two spouses who bring home work	Room for two home offices
Need to exercise in inclement weather	Room for exercise equipment
A stressful job	Isolated "quiet" room
Love of cooking	Versatile kitchen with pantry
Lot of stuff to store	Three-car garage
Lots of friends	Large dining and living room
Need to entertain professionally	Large dining and living room

What You Have (cont.)	*What You Need (cont.)*
Desire to stay home with family	Large family room
Two adults living together	Two master bedroom suites
Small children	Room for toys; sleeping area away from center of house
Children	Inside laundry room
Older children	Sound-isolated TV area
Desire to play outdoor games	Basketball or tennis courts, pool (try a condo)
Wood/metal tools you love to use	Oversized or three-car garage
Love of gardening	Large lot or hothouse (cold climate)
Need to be relaxed	Spa or space for sauna (try a condo)
Pet(s)	Fenced yard with easy access from both house and garage
Like to read	Many bookshelves, well-lit areas
Wet or snow environment	Mud room or changing room

TIP

Needs versus budget is always a delicate balancing act, but if you can afford any house at all, chances are you can afford one that is at least close to a golden fit. (Check out Chapter 6 for more details.)

TRAP

Beware of homes that have unusual or "freak" designs, such as round houses, or homes with only one huge room, or homes with many tiny rooms, or ones with very long, narrow kitchens—you get the idea. These may be offered to you for less and may fit your immediate needs, but they will be very difficult to resell later on and you'll have to lower your price to dump them.

These six tips will get you started. But there's a lot more to know in order to make a successful purchase. Read on.

2
Is Now the Right Time to Buy?

Is there a "right time" and a "wrong time" to buy a home?

Yes, there is.

Timing is critical; it can determine whether your purchase will be a financial success or failure. There are good and bad times of the year to buy and there are good markets and bad markets.

Let's begin with annual timing. The right time of the year to buy your home is in December, preferably during the last 2 weeks of the month when everyone is fussing about the holidays.

Historically, there are fewer home sales between Thanksgiving and New Year's (by a wide margin) than any other time of the year, simply because fewer buyers are out looking. Most buyers get involved with the holidays and put off home searching until after the new year. The last few weeks of December have the poorest sales of all.

Most sellers who haven't been able to sell their homes during the summer months feel the same way and remove them from the market after Thanksgiving. The only sellers who keep their homes up for sale (or list them at this time) are those who are desperate to get out. And if they haven't sold by the end of December, those sellers are very desperate, indeed.

There are so few buyers at the end of the year, in fact, that "motivated" sellers will often grab at ridiculously low offers just to get out of their property. If you want to save money, that's when you should make your offer. Buy your home in late December.

There's also a wrong time to buy. It's in late spring and early summer, specifically the months of April, May, and June. Historically speaking, between 30 and 35 percent of all homes (new and resales) will be sold during those 3 months. They are the peak selling times.

A big reason that April, May, and June are such good sales months has to do with school schedules. The school year is ending and families with children feel it is an optimum time to make a move. Also, families tend to be more financially optimistic in the spring and more willing to take the big step involved in a home purchase. Finally, it has to do with appearance. After the cold and/or wet winter, houses tend to look fresher and more appealing in spring. (Sellers, of course, know this and spruce up their places even more to lure buyers.)

If you want to pay top dollar, join the throngs of buyers and purchase in late spring and early summer. Otherwise, wait until the cold of December when you'll have better prices.

Is It a Seller's or a Buyer's Market?

Besides knowing the right time of the year to buy, it's also important to understand that the real estate market moves in cycles. Sometimes it's up, sometimes it's down. (It wasn't that long ago that people used to say, "Real estate is the only market that only goes up." How wrong they were!)

After the real estate market crash in the late 1980s and early 1990s, we all know (or should know) that home prices can go down too. Further, a declining market can last a long time—even half a decade or more.

Understanding this, you should use different strategies depending on the market's direction.

TIP

Just because it's a "buyer's market" doesn't mean it's a good time to buy. What it means is that savvy buyers may be staying out of the market.

Just Say "No!" When the Market Is Going Down

It may seem obvious, but the fact is that many of us time our purchase decision strictly with regard to our personal situation, without considering the market. For example:

- You may finally have the money saved up for a down payment.
- You need a bigger house to accommodate a growing family.
- You've moved into an area because of a job change and want a place to live.
- You've received an increase in salary and can now afford big home payments.

All of these are excellent reasons to buy a house, and many of us act on them. But none of these reasons takes into consideration market conditions. Yet buying a home is not like buying a refrigerator or even a car. You expect those items to decline in value as you use and enjoy them. But a home is also an investment, probably your biggest. Just as with stocks and bonds, you look forward to your home going up in value over time.

Therefore, beyond your personal motivation for buying, you must also consider the market.

If you buy when prices are going down, you may later find you can't sell for what you paid. (Millions of Americans found themselves in this unfortunate position during the early 1990s.) After years of paying taxes, carrying a big mortgage, and maintaining and repairing the property, you may discover that after commission and closing costs, it will cost money out of pocket to sell! Not an enviable position to be in.

TRAP

The trouble with a declining market is that you don't know, and no one can tell you, how far it will fall before it reaches bottom. If you buy on the way down, you will lose.

Therefore, if the market is declining, I suggest you rent, at least temporarily. While renting doesn't offer all the benefits of ownership, it does allow you to move out gracefully, without having to sell at a loss. And in any given area, there are usually many houses, condos, and townhouses always available for renting.

Besides, renting can be a lot cheaper than buying. Yes, as any real estate agent will tell you, there are financial advantages to home ownership, such as the ability to deduct property taxes and most mortgage interest from your income taxes. But these are usually more than offset by the higher costs of ownership, when compared with renting.

Often you can rent a home for far less than it costs to buy that same home. (In some areas, a house that costs an owner $2000 a month for mortgage payment, taxes, insurance, and maintenance can be rented for just about half to three-fourths of that amount—$1000 to $1500.)

In short, unless your property appreciates (increases annually in value), from a strictly dollars-and-sense perspective, you are probably better off renting temporarily until prices turn up.

TIP

If you otherwise qualify, you can deduct the expense of a home office from a rental just as well as from an owned home.

Buy When the Market Goes Up

Not quite as obvious. A rising market is often called a "seller's market." The reason is simple: There are many more buyers than sellers. Thus, the seller can raise prices—hence the term "seller's market."

You want to buy as soon as you see prices going up. Never mind that it's a seller's market and you'll have to pay more today than you could have for that same property last year. If prices are going up, the home you buy today will be worth even more next year and, hopefully, more still the year after that. You want to catch and ride the wave.

TIP

The reason buying a home is such an important financial investment to you is that it's one of the few places where you can safely leverage your money. If you put 10 percent down and the bank lends you 90 percent, you have leveraged the purchase by a ratio of 10 to 1. If the property value goes up by 5 percent, your investment has increased by 50 percent. (A $5000 increase on a $100,000 property is only 5 percent of the total cost. But if you invest only $10,000 as a down payment, it's 50 percent profit for you.) That's why you can't afford to stay out of real estate when the market's going up.

Remember, just as real estate is not the investment that always goes up, it's also not the investment that always declines. Sometimes the market will be so weak that you think it will last forever. That's another trap.

TRAP

Don't buy near the top. Too many people bought real estate in 1989 and 1990 just as the market reached its peak. At that time prices were appreciating at a remarkable 7 to 9 percent a year in most areas, and there were often multiple offers on a home as soon as it was offered for sale. Usually the market is ready to peak just when it's at its hottest.

How Do You Know When the Market Turns Around?

It's easy to tell. You can simply read the real estate articles in your local newspaper. As soon as there's an increase in the volume of sales and prices, it will be reported. Other media—including financial radio talk shows, TV news, and financial magazines—will report increases as well.

Or you can make contact with a real estate broker, announce that you want to wait until the market gets better, and ask for a call when there's a turnaround. (Just keep in mind that the agent's enthusiasm for a sale is likely to result in a call to you every time there's a blip in the market—confirm that it really is a turnaround by also keeping up with real estate news in the media, as noted above.)

It's probably also a good idea to keep checking back and occasionally calling other brokers as well. In a declining market, many brokers go out of business. (According to state licensing statistics, in California nearly a third of all real estate agents left the field during the declining market years between 1990 and 1995.)

TIP

Keep in mind that all real estate markets are regional. That means that while the market may be up in Illinois, it could be down in California; up in Arkansas, down in Massachusetts; and so on. Don't pay too much attention to national statistics. It's the market in your area that counts.

TRAP

Don't try to catch the exact turnaround. It's not necessary to buy a home at the very bottom of the market. When real estate turns around, it usually stays inexpensive for quite some time, often years, before prices begin climbing again. It's usually safe to buy when home prices have held stable for at least 9 months to a year.

What Are the Opportunities for Future Profits in Home Ownership?

They are excellent. It's only common sense that after the market has been down for a while, it's got nowhere else to go but up. Through the end of the 1990s we should see home values appreciate across the country. Of course, that doesn't mean there won't be pockets where values will remain stagnant or even decline. But overall, the last half of the decade should be very good for real estate, indeed.

And you should be participating in the profits.

3
Everything Is Negotiable!

This whole chapter is just one tip and here it is: *Everything is negotiable when buying a house.* The trouble is that most buyers either don't believe it or don't like it.

Here's a *partial* list of what's negotiable when you buy a house:

- Price
- Financing
- Closing costs (except where specified by law)
- Occupancy (when you get the key and can move in)
- Painting (will the seller repaint a portion of or the entire house?)
- Repairs (will the seller repair the roof, plumbing, windows, and so on, and what kind and quality of repairs will be made?)
- Yard (will the seller remove unwanted trees or bushes, or put in desired landscaping?)
- Fixtures (which lights, fans, and appliances stay and which go?)
- Wall coverings (do the drapes stay or go?)
- Doghouse (does it go or stay?)
- Dog or cat (does it stay?)
- Furniture (will the seller throw in certain pieces?)

- Prepaid taxes and insurance (will the seller credit you with these?)
- And *everything else!*

Custom suggests that in certain areas certain things are paid for by the buyer and others by the seller (such as title insurance or escrow costs) or that certain items (such as personal property) do not go with the house. Even so, you can throw custom to the winds. Everything, with only rare exceptions, is up for grabs when you buy a home. How much you grab for yourself and how much the seller grabs depends on how well you negotiate.

Of course, that's the rub. Many of us feel at a loss as negotiators. In the back of our minds we know we're going to come out second best and we just don't want to bother. That's the trap.

Negotiation gives the buyer incredible power in making a favorable transaction. It can also place him or her in a position of immense weakness. The fact is that how you negotiate determines whether you get the home of your dreams—or whether those dreams end up being a nightmare.

Do You Negotiate from Weakness?

I once had a friend who had an absolute abhorrence for traveling in Mexico, even though her business obligations required that she routinely go there. "Why?" I asked her on one occasion. "Why don't you like traveling in Mexico? The people are friendly. The scenery in many areas is spectacular. And the currency exchange rate for Americans is almost always very favorable. So, what don't you like about it?"

She glowered at me for a moment, then replied, "You never know what the price of anything is in Mexico." She waited for that to sink in, then continued, "You want to buy a pair of shoes. The price written on them may be 200 pesos. But you know you should be able to get them for about half, probably 100 pesos.

"You try to bargain and the seller gets upset and starts yelling, accusing you of trying to steal food from the mouths of his children. He says you're trying to cheat him and demands the full price. It gets embarrassing. I end up being upset and I don't enjoy myself. Why don't they just ask for 100 pesos to begin with?"

I nodded understandingly and said, "But don't you see? The negotiation for the price is a kind of ritual. It's anticipated that you'll offer less and pay less than the asking price. The seller's insults and threats are just a way of doing business, trying to get you to pay more. *There's nothing personal in it.*"

She nodded, "Maybe that's why I feel so embarrassed when I end up paying 200 pesos for a pair of 100 peso shoes."

I told my friend not to take it so *personally*. I indicated that when I'd visited Mexico I'd seen a buyer and seller haggle for nearly an hour over the price of some small trinket, hurling accusations of thievery and insults relating to family origin. All the hostility was immediately forgotten the moment the sale was concluded, at which time both buyer and seller embraced each other as though they were bosom buddies. "Negotiation for price and even terms of sale is the accepted practice in probably 75 percent of the world. It is an ancient and honored tradition."

My friend scowled at me. "It's not a tradition in the United States. When I go into a department store, I know what the price is. There are no shenanigans, no arguing, no negotiations. If a pair of shoes in Macy's is listed at $65, that's the price—no ifs, ands, or buts!"

It was the end of our conversation. My friend was absolutely convinced that negotiating was the bane of third world countries—that it had no place in societies such as our own.

How wrong she was.

Negotiation for price or terms of sale always has been and always will be the *rule* in any capitalist society. The appearance of fixed prices found in stores in the United States and other industrialized countries is simply a thin veneer of marketing. Most stores from groceries to clothing are simply outlets for manufacturer's products. Each store represents a price level. If you don't like that price level, then try the store across the street—or your neighborhood discounter, or superdiscounter, or manufacturer's outlet, or mail-order dealer. The price for almost any product will vary depending on the store you are in.

In the United States, where unskilled sales clerks are often the rule, the prices are set per store as a convenience, not to you the buyer, but to the seller. Want a different price? Go to a different store. Where skilled sales personnel are employed, as in auto dealerships, negotiation is as alive in this country as it is in the heart of Mexico.

How Do You Negotiate in Real Estate?

Which brings us back to buying a home. Here, as we've seen, everything is negotiable—the most important items usually being the price and the terms. If you're a good negotiator, you may end up paying as much as 15 percent or more below what the seller is asking.

Negotiation is an inherent part of buying real estate and if you're going to participate, you should plan on learning the basic skills.

Should You Rely on the Agent?

At this point, I'm sure some readers are saying, "Hold on. I worked with an agent when I bought my last home. The agent did my negotiating. The agent saw that I got a good price."

I doubt it. I doubt it very seriously. You may have gotten a good price, but if you did, it was largely because of your own efforts. The agent in most cases is the *seller's* agent, with a fiduciary responsibility to the seller to find a buyer. In most states it is unethical if not outright illegal for the seller's agent to even suggest that you offer less than the seller is asking!

This doesn't mean that agents don't, in fact, do so. In my experience many agents do. But they often couch their suggestions in language such as, "The sellers have indicated that they are anxious to sell and that they'd be agreeable to an offer of a little less than the asking price."

Indeed. The sellers may be desperate and may be willing to take an offer of 25 percent less than the asking price. But the agent can't come right out and tell you that, because in most cases she represents the seller. In addition, the agent doesn't really want you to make a low offer. The lower your offer, the harder it is for the agent to get the seller to accept and the less chance there is of getting a commission. (The agent normally gets a commission only when there's a sale.) On the other hand, if you offer just a *little bit less,* sure the seller would accept that in a flash. The agent would be thrilled to make such an easy commission.

So instead of offering $25,000 less than the asking price, you offer $5000 less—and get it. The seller is happy. The agent's happy. And you, you big dummy, are happy because you think you got yourself a "good price."

The point is that you can't rely on anyone but yourself when it comes to negotiation. A good agent can handle the actual mechanics of speaking for you to the seller, and that's certainly a big plus. But it's ultimately up to you to determine what the parameters of the negotiation are going to be. You set the price, the terms, and all the other conditions of sale that you will accept. (Also see Chapter 7 for picking a good agent.)

Are You Your Own Worst Enemy?

Which brings us back to you. Most house hunters, particularly house hunters who don't regularly invest in real estate, are worried about hurting the seller's feelings, about insulting the agent by offering a price far lower than the asking price, and most important, about doing anything that would appear foolish.

If that's the way you feel when you open negotiations for the purchase of your next home, you are a gone goose.

Remember the example of buying shoes in Mexico? The seller and buyer in third world countries often trade insults for a very long time, haggling over the price. But then, when it's all said and done, they shake hands and become bosom buddies.

Well, you may not end up bosom buddies with the seller, but remember that when negotiating for real estate you are participating in that same age-old ritual of bargaining. You are back there under the tent in the wilderness relying on your own cleverness and personal will power.

If you are weak and susceptible to the influence of the seller (or the seller's agent), you could be talked into paying a higher price, getting less favorable terms, or (worst of all) accepting a house that you really don't want. On the other hand, if you are a good "horse trader" you are going to get a good deal all around.

Can I Negotiate on a New House?

A few exceptions are in order here. Sometimes you're buying a brand new home instead of a resale. The builder/developer has a set price written in ink on the brochure. Either you pay that price, you are told, or you don't get the home. Right?

It depends. If the market is hot and new homes are selling as fast as they can be put up, yes, you'll have to pay the set price. In fact, I can recall a few years ago when the market was very hot when people would camp out in front of builder/developers' offices for days just for the privilege of paying full price for a new home!

On the other hand, if the market is slow, there's no reason you can't offer a builder/developer a lower price—and get it. (Just remember that builder/developers often have a relatively small profit margin and they may not be able to accept a severely reduced price. See Chapter 16 on buying a brand new home from a builder/developer.)

Should You Negotiate Directly with the Seller?

Sometimes sellers will bypass the use of an agent and attempt to sell their homes themselves. (In the trade these are called FSBOs—for sale by owners.) The temptation is to think that because no agent is involved, the seller doesn't have to pay a commission and, hence, can offer a lower price.

Maybe. On the other hand, you now not only have to set the parameters of your negotiations (price and terms) but also have to carry those negotiations out face to face.

If you're a good horse trader and if the seller is too, things should go fine and no agent may be needed. But, unfortunately, in our country most people have been inured into thinking in terms of fixed prices and not negotiation. Hence, when you offer the seller far less than he or she is asking, you could be asked to leave in not so pleasant terms and further negotiations may be impossible.

Or, if the seller is a good negotiator and you aren't, when your low offer is rejected along with suggestions that you've insulted the seller's integrity, you may be put off and leave without realizing that it was all part of the game.

As a result, for the vast majority of people, buying direct from sellers (contrary to what the TV "get rich quick" gurus of real estate push) is more difficult, and less likely to result in a good price and terms, than dealing with a broker/agent. (I'll have a lot more to say about working with a broker/agent in later chapters.)

Can You Learn to Negotiate Successfully?

In the old days in real estate (by old days I mean as late as the 1950s) the Latin expression "caveat emptor" was often quoted: "Let the buyer beware."

Since that time, consumer protection laws have swelled to the point where today the buyer who knows how to take advantage of these laws is protected and even has advantages as never before. However, when it comes to the actual negotiations, there are no protections for the buyer. You are at your own mercy. You can make a good deal. Or you can get yourself into terrible trouble.

The question naturally arises, therefore, of how a person who is not a real estate professional can negotiate successfully in what may be a den of wolves. How do you avoid cheating yourself by your negotiation inexperience?

The answer is by acquiring knowledge. Having read this chapter thus far, you've already acquired a great deal that you may not have known before. You now know that everything is negotiable. When the agent says, "There's no way you can ask for the refrigerator. It's personal property and goes with the seller automatically." You can stand back, catch your breath, and say with confidence, "Either I get that damn refrigerator or there's no deal!"

Grumbling, the agent will write into the contract that the refrigerator goes with the house, knowing full well that he or she is going to have to fight the sellers for hours to get them to agree.

You should now know that there's nothing embarrassing about submitting low offers and making your agent struggle to get the seller to sign. There's nothing wrong with insisting on terms which are totally favorable to you. You should also now know that it's a mistake to let the seller's agent "assist" you in determining the price to offer.

Finally, you should now know that there's nothing foolish about getting down on the ground and scrambling for price and terms. It's an ancient tradition that, regardless of your particular background, is your human heritage. You were born to do it!

Knowledge Is Power

Ultimately, how you fare when buying a home is going to be a direct result of the knowledge you have. The more you know, the better a position you'll be in to negotiate from strength.

How do you get that knowledge? In the next chapters you will find exposed those common and not so common traps that most buyers fall into. You'll also be given tips on what to look for and how to find exactly what you want in a home. Perhaps for the first time in your house-hunting experience, you will have a tool in hand that is completely dedicated to working for you. The following information aims to see that you get what you want when you buy a home. (You'll find no sympathy for agents, sellers, lenders, or others you need to deal with here.) You might also check out my book *Tips and Traps When Negotiating Real Estate* (McGraw-Hill, 1995).

There is only one way to negotiate and that is to negotiate from strength. There is only one way to get strength: through knowledge. Read on.

4
Do I Really Need a Big Down Payment?

Most people who want to buy a home find that the single biggest roadblock is coming up with the cash down payment. (So if you're feeling the pinch, rest assured you're not alone!)

Let's face it, we live in a credit society. A family with a $100,000 annual income can easily obtain a new car loan with almost nothing down and a $500-a-month car payment. But that same family may not have $5000 in the bank in a savings account. In fact, over 80 percent of all families have little or no cash savings. (On the other hand, that other 20 percent or so have whopping big savings accounts. I guess a lot has to do with priorities.)

I'm reminded of that old saw about the two investors who want to buy the Empire State Building in New York. The first investor, just returned from a meeting with the sellers, tells the second, "I've got good news and bad. The good news is that they'll take our $500 million offer."

"Great," says the second investor. "What's the bad news?"

"They want $500 cash down!"

Should You Look for a Lower Down Payment?

Wanting to buy a house and faced with the prospect of having to come up with a cash down payment, many buyers embark on a search for the highest possible mortgage. After all, the higher the mortgage, the less cash you need to put into the property.

Unfortunately, such buyers sometimes get in over their heads with higher interest and payments than they can really afford. This can eventually result in their losing the property to foreclosure. Yes, you want a low-down, high-mortgage purchase. But you don't want payments so stiff that they'll smother you.

In this chapter we'll take a look at your down payment alternatives. We'll see how you can reduce the down you're required to pay *almost* to nothing. On the other hand, we'll also look at the risks involved in doing just that.

TRAP

Don't even dream about "no money down" purchases. With certain rare exceptions, they never have existed as economically realistic alternatives. The whole concept was dreamed up by marketers to sell books, tapes, and seminars.

Why Do You Need a Down Payment at All?

If banks are willing to lend you 80 percent of the purchase price of a home, why don't they just go ahead and lend you the whole 100 percent? I mean, they're banks, aren't they? Are they short of money and unable to come up with the other 20 percent, or what?!

Actually, in the vast majority of cases, when you get a mortgage, the lender, be it a bank, savings and loan, mortgage banker/broker, or some other institution, has to follow underwriting guidelines that prescribe both a down payment and its size. Think of it this way. The lender you deal with lends only a tiny portion of the mortgage that you get. Ninety-five percent or more *of your loan* comes from a behind-the-scenes or "secondary" source. This secondary source is usually a government-sponsored organization such as

Fannie Mae or Freddie Mac. Or it could be a fund composed of insurance companies or other savings and loans and banks from another part of the country. Sometimes it's even money from foreign investors.

TIP

Money is money. It shouldn't matter to you whether yours came from California, Vermont, or Tokyo. But knowing the constraints that your lender feels may help you arrange a more comfortable loan.

Where the Money Comes from When You Get a Mortgage

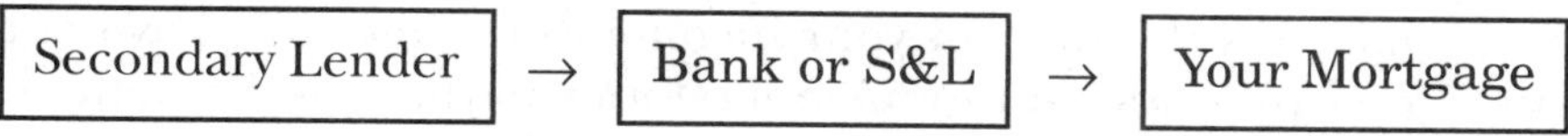

What's important to remember is that the secondary lenders' underwriting requirements say that you must come up with a healthy down payment. You don't come up with the down, your bank or savings and loan can't meet the underwriting requirements and in turn will turn you down.

Why Do Secondary Lenders Want You to Put Money Down?

It's all a matter of risk. Remember, secondary lenders are at risk for 95 percent of your mortgage. They don't want you to default (not make the payments). And history has shown that the more money a buyer puts into a property, the less likely he or she is to walk away and stop making mortgage payments. In other words, lenders want you to have something to lose. The more of your own money is in the deal, the more motivated you will be to see that everything works out successfully. (On the other hand, if you have nothing in the pot, you won't care that much if the pot tips over.)

How Much Is a "Standard" Down Payment?

That's an easy question to answer. Underwriters universally feel that you should put 20 percent down. You put one-fifth into the property and the mortgage will be four-fifths. That's a formula that over the years has proved highly successful. With that much in, you'll do almost anything to keep that property afloat, including making mortgage payments no matter what happens.

On the other hand, secondary lenders realize that few people in this country actually have 20 percent to put down. So they have an alternate plan. They'll let you put only 10 percent down (you come up with one-tenth and the loan will be nine-tenths). But, in order to get this preferential treatment, you must be a "better borrower."

What's a better borrower? Today that's defined by a complex formula that tests the ratio of your income to the monthly payment (the lower the ratio—more income/lower payment—the better), your credit history, your job security, and so on. It's all done on a computer. Go into a lender and in a few minutes you'll be told how big a monthly payment you can qualify for and whether you'll have to come up with 20 percent or 10 percent down payment.

10% Down	20% Down
90% Mortgage	80% Mortgage

How Do I Get a Higher Mortgage and a Lower Down?

With all this said, it's important to be aware that there are alternatives. Some lenders you deal with may not work with underwriters. They may put up all the money you borrow themselves and, for a higher interest rate, may consider a lower down payment. Other lenders may work with more lenient private underwriters who may also allow a lower down payment. And there are also low-down government-sponsored loans as well as private mortgage insurance to ease the down. We'll cover each separately. (Don't get confused yet. Wait until a later chapter when we talk about different types of mortgages that are available!)

TIP

Mortgages that conform to government underwriting guidelines are called *conforming* loans. They have a maximum loan amount which changes periodically. (At this writing, it was $207,000.) All other private mortgages are called *nonconforming* loans.

TRAP

Some nonconforming mortgages are called *jumbos* because they have a higher dollar amount than conforming loans offer. Most jumbos, however, require that you qualify for the loan as if it were conforming in all other ways. In other words, you need sterling credit and a standard down payment. However, in order to get a higher mortgage amount, the lender will charge you a slightly higher interest rate—usually ½ to 1 percent higher—than for a conforming loan. Jumbos do not usually offer you a lower down payment, just a higher loan.

What Is Private Mortgage Insurance?

If you have an excellent credit history and if the house itself qualifies (is in a good neighborhood in good condition and is considered "prime" by lenders), you may be able to get private mortgage insurance (PMI). This insures the lender (not you) against loss in case you default. With PMI you may need to put only as little as 5 percent down.

PMI insurance, however, adds an additional ¼ to ½ or more percent in interest to your mortgage. Almost any bank or savings and loan can arrange a PMI loan.

What Are Portfolio Lenders?

Another alternative is to secure financing from a savings and loan or other lending institution which carries its own portfolio. (In other words, instead of dealing with a secondary lender and underwriting, it loans the money itself.) A portfolio lender lends the whole mortgage, takes all the risk, and gets all the interest.

Portfolio lenders are allowed by government regulation to reduce the down payment on a small percentage of their total loans to as low as 5 percent (although most don't do this). Thus, if you can find a portfolio lender, you maybe able to secure a lower down payment.

TIP

How do you find a portfolio lender? Call. Get your phone book, look up banks, savings and loan associations (also called thrift associations in some parts of the country), and start calling. Ask to talk to the loan officers. Ask if they make 5 or 10 percent down payment loans. If they do, they'll let you know immediately. Another way to find portfolio lenders is to contact a local real estate broker. In most urban areas, brokers receive weekly lists of all lenders indicating their requirements and their offerings, including down payment. A broker with such a list can immediately tell which lender is offering what in terms of down payment and interest rates that week.

What About Government-Assisted Financing?

There are several government programs available. Probably the most well known is the FHA (Federal Housing Administration) loan on single-family dwellings. The FHA insures a private lender under this program and the down payment may be as low as 5 percent. The trouble with FHA loans is that they tend to have lower maximum mortgage amounts (compared to conforming loans). In addition, they require you to have excellent credit and to live in the home.

TRAP

FHA loans were extremely popular at one time. Because the FHA has had to take back enormous numbers of properties through foreclosure over the last few years, however, it has tightened up its requirements. One of these requirements is that the borrower pay the insurance fee for the loan up front. (In the past this fee could be paid monthly over the life of the loan.) The fee can be quite substantial.

TIP

To make the inclusion of an insurance fee more palatable, the FHA has been allowing lenders to add the fee to the loan amount. You still pay it over the life of the mortgage, but at least it doesn't have to be in cash out of your pocket.

The Veterans Administration (VA) also has a program which guarantees loans to lenders. It offers true "nothing down" financing, but again these are for relatively low mortgage amounts. To qualify, you must be a veteran who served during certain specified periods. You must also meet strict requirements. Since the times of service change fairly regularly, as do the actual requirements, you should contact the Veterans Administration to determine if you would qualify for a VA loan.

What About Seller Financing?

Finally, there is always the seller. Often a seller will be willing to carry a second mortgage (or other level of mortgage) in order to make the sale. You may be able to secure an 80 percent mortgage from an institutional lender (bank, savings and loan, and so on) and then get another 10 or 15 percent from the seller in the form of a carry-back (second) mortgage.

5–10% Down payment
10–15% Seller's second mortgage
80% Mortgage from lender

TRAP

The impetus behind much of the "no money down" nonsense that was popularized in real estate a few years ago was to get sellers to carry back all the down payment—20 percent or sometimes even more! The sellers were placed at a real disadvantage in terms of collateral, and today few if any sellers are foolish enough to consider this. In addition, most institutional lenders will not offer a mortgage unless you put down at least 10 percent of your own money. (No more than a 10 percent second on an 80 percent first.) To get around this, a few unscrupulous real estate people suggested lying to the institutional lender and securing a 20 percent (or more!) second mortgage "under the table" from the seller. Yes, it can and has been done. But you as a buyer open yourself to enormous liability if you participate in such a scheme. Most institutional lenders are federally insured, and that means that if word ever gets out, the federal government (Treasury or FBI) investigates. Enough said that the penalties for securing a mortgage under fraud are quite severe.

Are There Any Other Practical Alternatives?

These, then, are your main alternatives with regard to a down payment. Suffice it to say you will need some payment. How much you will need depends on how tenacious and inventive you are in locating lenders willing to make higher-percentage loans. But the fact remains that you will still need to get money for the down payment (not to mention the closing costs).

Where will that money come from?

It would be nice if we could simply write out a check. However, most of us are always pressed for cash. Other than a flush checking or savings account, here are some sources of cash for a down payment which you may not have considered before.

Possible Sources of Cash for the Down Payment

1. Cash value of life insurance (borrowing on it)
2. Refinancing or selling an auto or boat
3. Sale of other physical assets to generate cash
4. Sale of stocks, bonds, or other securities
5. Sale of present home
6. Gifts or loans from relatives or friends
7. Refinancing investment real estate you already own (must be obtained before applying for the loan)
8. Income tax refund
9. Letter of credit or credit line from a bank (must be obtained before applying for the loan)
10. MasterCard, Visa, or other credit card (must be obtained before applying for the loan)
11. "Sweat equity"—offering to fix up a house in return for a reduced down payment
12. Accumulation of funds from your regular income between date of purchase and close of escrow (insist on a long escrow—3 months or more)
13. Personal loan on hobby materials, jewelry or furs, cameras, or other property.

14. Business loan (must be obtained before applying for the loan)
15. Passbook loan (must be obtained before applying for the loan)

TRAP

Many of the sources of cash listed involve borrowing. However, a requirement of all government-insured lenders is that the down payment not come from borrowed funds. If you indicate that you are borrowing the down payment, it is almost certain to disqualify you from normal financing.

TIP

Borrow the money at least 3 months before you enter into a transaction to purchase a home. That way, you'll have the cash in hand and borrowing will show up as an existing loan against your credit, not new borrowing. Be aware, however, that an extra loan against your credit could decrease the amount you could borrow on a home. (You will be tying up some of your income to pay off the loan. That income won't be available to help you qualify for a home mortgage.)

What About Closing Costs?

Most buyers simply overlook this very real cost. Don't. Closing costs are expensive. Typically they are around 5 percent of the purchase price of the house. If you pay $100,000 for a home, expect to pay about $5000 in closing costs.

These are cash costs. You need to come up with them *in addition* to your down payment. They include:

- Points (percentage of the mortgage paid to the lender to compensate for a lower interest rate or for the "work" of making the loan)
- Title and escrow charges
- Document fees

- Attorney fees
- Other costs

We'll examine closing costs much more closely in Chapter 12.

There are several methods of reducing, eliminating, or deferring closing costs. One is to have the mortgage amount increased to cover the closing costs. Check with your lender to see if it can be done. Another option is to negotiate the closing costs with the seller before you commit to the purchase. Remember, closing costs are negotiable. You and the seller can agree between yourselves that as part of the deal the seller will pay your closing costs. What's the chances of a seller agreeing? Pretty good in a buyer's market where the seller is desperate to unload a house. Not so good in a seller's market where houses are moving rapidly.

Also, keep in mind that negotiability extends to all areas of the transaction. If you're getting a terrific price, the seller is less inclined to pay part or all of your closing costs. On the other hand, if you're giving the seller pretty much what he or she wants in price and the market isn't too tight, then reduced closing costs may be possible.

5
How to Qualify for a Bigger Mortgage

All of us want to know the top price we can afford to pay for a home. Unfortunately, the maximum price is irrelevant. What counts is the maximum mortgage that we can get. The reason is simple. Unless you're one of the lucky few who can pay cash, the bigger the mortgage, the more you can afford to pay for a home—bigger mortgage, bigger price.

How big a mortgage can you qualify for?

It's very important that you answer this question before you do any serious house hunting. After all, why waste your time looking at $200,000 homes when the most you can afford is a $150,000 house? On the other hand, why sell yourself short looking at only $125,000 places when you can afford better? You can't realistically house-hunt until you know how big a house you can buy. And you won't know that until you know how big a mortgage you can get.

TIP

There are no price restrictions, only mortgage restrictions. Remember, the tendency when buying is to think only in terms of price: How high a price can I afford? A better way to look at it is: How big a mortgage can I afford?

There are a several ways to determine just how big a mortgage you can really afford.

What Is Prequalifying?

A popular technique in recent years is to ask for prequalifying interviews with lenders. Essentially this means that you contact a lender such as a savings and loan or a bank before you go house hunting. A loan officer then does a screening interview. The screening interview usually takes one of two forms: informal and formal.

The Informal Screening

Informal screening usually takes 10 minutes or less. You tell the lender what you make, how much money you have in the bank, and what your credit is like. The lender does some quick calculations on the computer and tells you how much money you can get on various kinds of mortgages toward the purchase of a home. (See Chapter 18 for different mortgage types.)

The problem here is that you "can't take it to the bank." This informal bit of information carries no weight with sellers or with agents. They may just nod affably and go on to something else. It's nothing more than an opinion; it has no negotiating value.

TRAP

In an informal screening, you may exaggerate. You may not even know the true answers to some of the questions asked and may guess at them—and end up being quite inaccurate. On the other hand, the lender is in no way committed to anything she may say. In other words, the whole interview is an exercise in fantasizing. Yes, you may get a ballpark figure for how much of a loan you can get and, therefore, how big a house you can afford. But chances are you could be off so significantly that it could lead you to search for either a house that is too high in price for you or one that offers far less in the amenities you want.

The Formal Screening

Formal screening takes longer. Here you go to a specific lender (or to a mortgage broker who qualifies you with a specific lender). The lender takes a written loan application from you. In it you are asked to fill out information on every aspect of your financial life, going back a good many years. Some of the questions may seem personal. They are. Just grin and bear it. If you want the money, you have to bare your soul.

Once the application is in, the lender may ask for money. You may be asked to come up with around $50 (usually less) for a credit report.

TRAP

Never pay for a mortgage before you get it. During times when interest rates are low and lots of borrowers want mortgages, some unscrupulous lenders ask for thousands of dollars up front. If the lender asks for more than $50, for example, for prepaid points or document fees or other costs—run, don't walk, out of the office. You're being had. On the other hand, a very few lenders pick up the fee for the credit report themselves.

After you pay the credit report cost and turn in the completed and signed mortgage application, you may (rarely) be asked for additional documents such as 2 years of tax returns (if you're self-employed) or signed statements from banks showing your deposits or from your employer showing your job status. You'll have to turn these in anyway if you end up getting the loan. Most lenders make a commitment assuming that what you've told them is accurate, but some still do insist on actually seeing the documents.

Finally, usually a day or so later, you'll be notified of the size of loan you qualify for from your formal screening and be given a letter. This is a fairly hard commitment. You can usually bank on it. Now you can seriously go house hunting.

TIP

Formal screening to prequalify is extremely useful in a competitive market in which houses are selling fast. You are at an advantage over other buyers if you can go into negotiations with your financing already arranged. You may beat out an equally qualified buyer who doesn't have financing in hand.

TRAP

Prequalifying means only that you are assured of a mortgage from that particular lender. It may turn out that some other lender may offer better terms. Unless speed is of the essence, you are usually better off waiting until after you have signed a purchase agreement and had it accepted by the seller to look for final financing. You increase your chances of getting the best financing terms this way. (Normally you'll put a contingency clause in the purchase contract that allows you out of the deal in the event you can't find financing. It's discussed in Chapter 9.)

Can I Qualify Myself?

Thus far we have considered only how a lender may qualify you for a mortgage. However, you don't have to go to a lender for this. If you know the parameters you can just as quickly and easily qualify yourself. That's what we're going to do now. (*Note:* The following requires some simple math—percentages, addition, subtraction, and such. If such calculating is a problem for you, stick with getting qualified by a lender.)

To begin, fill out the following simple worksheet. It's to qualify for a standard conforming loan. (See Chapter 4 if you're not sure what a conforming loan is.)

Your Mortgage Worksheet

Determining Your Maximum Monthly Payment

Your combined monthly gross income	$ 2500
Less any long-term debt (car payments, credit cards, etc.)	− 100
Monthly total	$ 2400
Multiply by .33 (for an 80% loan)	× 792
Multiply by .28 (for a 90% loan)	× 672
Maximum monthly payment you can afford	$
Less insurance and taxes on the property (annual amount divided by 12)	−
Maximum monthly mortgage payment you can afford	

The worksheet is deceptively simple and surprisingly accurate. The answer you get should give you a fairly close figure to what a lender would come up with. For example, here's how a typical couple might answer the worksheet.

Your Mortgage Worksheet

Determining Your Maximum Monthly Payment

Your combined gross income	$3000
Less any long-term debt (car payments)	−270
Monthly total	$2730
Multiply by .33 (for an 80% loan)	$901
Multiply by .28 (for a 90% loan)	$742
Maximum monthly payment you can afford	$901 or $742
Less insurance and taxes on the property (annual amount divided by 12)	−$150
Maximum monthly mortgage payment you can afford	= $751 or $592

Do You Understand the Chart?

Here are the definitions you need for the terms used:

Combined income. This is both spouses' gross income. It is the total on your paystub *before* taxes and other deductions.

Long-term debt. This is any debt that is going to take you more than 6 months to pay off. It includes credit cards.

TIP

If you want to raise the mortgage amount you can qualify for (and hence the purchase price), pay off credit card and other long-term debt first. For example, you may owe eight more installments on your washing machine. Pay off three installments. Now you only owe five. For many lenders, it has changed from long-term to short-term debt.

Multiply by .33 or .28. These arcane-sounding numbers are figures that lenders use to determine your ability to repay. Typically, you can't afford (according to lenders) to have a mortgage for more than 28 percent of your gross income (if it's 90 percent of the purchase price) or 33 percent of your gross income (if it's 80 percent of the purchase price).

TRAP

Don't believe it for a minute! People who are good money managers can handle debts as high as 50 percent. Bad money managers can't handle debts as low as 20 percent. The .28 and .33 numbers lenders use came out of studies done for the Federal Housing Administration in the 1930s and 1940s. They are arbitrary. (The easiest way to recognize this fact is to ask why the same person could afford 34 percent of gross income on an 80 percent loan while only 28 percent on a 90 percent loan? Shouldn't you be able to afford a set amount regardless of the size of the loan?) The reason for the percentages lies in the risk to the lender. Presumably at 28 percent, you are more easily able to make the payment and less of a risk. Nonsense! But it's nonsense you must abide by in order to get a lender to give you an institutional mortgage.

Taxes and insurance. Before calculating the final mortgage payment you can afford, you must take into account taxes and insurance. If you already have a property in mind, find out from the owner, agent, or county assessor what the taxes *will be* when you buy. Find out what the insurance amount will be from an insurance agent. Usually these are given annually. Divide by 12 to get the monthly amount.

TRAP

Don't rely on the current tax or insurance bill. In many states, property is reassessed when it is sold (Proposition 13 in California). That means that your property will have a new assessed valuation and, more than likely, higher taxes when you become owner. Also, the present owner may not be insuring the property for full value. You'll want to do that, so your insurance bill could well be higher.

TIP

If you haven't found a property yet, use the following guesstimates for taxes. (First figure the maximum house price you can afford, as shown below.)

In states with low taxes—1–2 percent of house price

In states with medium taxes—3 percent of house price

In states with high taxes—4 percent of house price

Any agent, escrow officer, loan officer, real estate lawyer, and many others can tell you whether you live in a high-, medium-, or low-tax state.

What's the Maximum Mortgage I Can Afford?

Be sure you understand this clearly. Thus far we've been calculating the maximum monthly payment. (No, this is not necessarily the maximum payment you can afford in reality. It's the maximum payment that lenders think you can afford.)

Once you know the maximum payment that you can afford, it's relatively simple to determine the maximum mortgage. The attached chart gives mortgages for various interest rates based on the monthly payment. (The chart works backward—usually you know the mortgage amount and then use the chart to determine the monthly payment. Here we know the monthly payment and from it are deriving the maximum mortgage.)

Table 5.1. Finding Your Maximum Mortgage

To use the chart, locate the maximum payment you can afford on the left side. Once you have found your maximum payment, read across the top of the chart to the current interest rate. Where the current interest rate intersects with the maximum payment you can afford you will find the approximate mortgage you can afford. (Assumes 30-year loan.) For higher monthly payments, add payments and mortgage amounts together.

Monthly payment you can afford	Current interest rate for mortgage loan			
	7%	8%	9%	10%
$ 300	$ 45,092	$ 40,885	$ 37,284	$ 34,185
$ 400	$ 60,123	$ 54,513	$ 49,712	$ 45,580
$ 500	$ 75,154	$ 68,142	$ 62,140	$ 56,975
$ 600	$ 90,185	$ 81,770	$ 74,568	$ 68,370
$ 700	$105,215	$ 95,398	$ 86,995	$ 79,765
$ 800	$120,246	$104,027	$ 99,423	$ 91,160
$ 900	$135,277	$122,655	$111,851	$102,555
$1,000	$150,308	$136,283	$124,279	$113,950

How Do I Determine the Maximum House Price I Can Afford?

Once again we work backward. Usually we know the price of the house and then calculate the maximum mortgage. Typically it is 80 or 90 percent of the house price.

Table 5.2. Finding Your Maximum Price

Find your maximum monthly payment on left, the interest rate on mortgage across the top. Where the two figures meet is the *approximate* maximum price you can afford. For higher monthly payments add payments and mortgage amounts together.

Monthly payment	Interest Rate			
	6%	7%	8%	9%
300	55,000	50,000	46,000	43,000
400	74,000	67,000	61,000	56,000
500	92,000	83,000	76,000	65,000
600	110,000	100,000	91,000	84,000
700	129,000	117,000	107,000	98,000
800	147,000	134,000	122,000	112,000
900	166,000	150,000	137,000	126,000
1,000	184,000	167,000	153,000	140,000

Chart assumes a fixed-rate, 30-year mortgage, 20 percent down payment, and taxes and insurance of 1¾ percent annually.

Can I Get a "Better Loan?"

You may be able to avoid the severe restrictions noted by getting an equity loan from some lenders. This is a type of portfolio mortgage in which the lender itself carries all of the money loaned. Only the loans are typically for less—usually not more than 75 percent of the value of the property—and nobody cares how much you make or what you can qualify for! The only consideration is that the property appraise for high enough to justify the mortgage.

But beware. Equity loans have higher interest rates and often shorter terms. Private portfolio banks and thrifts sometimes make these loans, but for the most part they are made by private mortgage lenders. Check your phone book under Mortgage Lenders.

TRAP

Private mortgage lenders are usually private individuals or groups of individuals who are very familiar with the real estate business and who are willing to take risks. While they must have a real estate license and sometimes a mortgage broker's license in most states and must abide by many rules and regulations, they are not nearly as well regulated as banks and savings and loans. In addition, they don't have the fancy stone buildings and the highly visible images to protect. Consequently, they may try to stick you with extra costs, higher than necessary interest rates, and other restrictive or undesirable mortgage terms. When dealing with a private mortgage lender, always have a real estate attorney working on your side. (*Note:* Don't confuse mortgage lenders with mortgage brokers, who often retail loans for banks and savings and loans; they don't lend money themselves and usually don't make equity loans.)

Can I Get a Lower Interest Rate?

What should be obvious is that the amount of mortgage you can afford for any given payment rapidly goes down as the interest rate you have to pay goes up. For example, if you can afford $1000 a month, at 9 percent you can afford roughly a $125,000 mortgage. However, at 15 percent you can afford only about an $80,000 mortgage, all at the same monthly payment.

The interest rate on the mortgage is not something you have a whole lot of control over. The cost of borrowing money fluctuates widely, and a lot depends on the timing of your purchase. As recently as 1988, interest rates on owner-occupied homes had risen to almost 12 percent. At the time this book was written, they had dropped back down to around 7 or 8 percent.

If interest rates are high when you decide to buy, one alternative is an adjustable-rate mortgage. Typically these offer low initial interest rates as an inducement to make the purchase. Thus far we have been considering only fixed-interest rates (which are the true interest rate). For adjustable mortgages, this rate may be considerably lower.

For example, at a time when fixed rates are at 8 percent, it is not uncommon for adjustable rates to be at 6 or even 5 percent. Think of how much bigger a mortgage and how much bigger a house you can afford with an adjustable at 5 percent than with a fixed-rate mortgage at 8 percent!

It's not quite that easy. In the past, lenders allowed buyers to qualify at their initial low "teaser" rates for adjustable loans. However, this resulted in many foreclosures when the adjustable rates rose and buyers couldn't make the payments. Today most lenders qualify buyers somewhere between their initial teaser rate for an adjustable loan and the fixed rate. For example, if the fixed rate is 7 percent and the adjustable rate is 5 percent, you may be required to qualify at 6 percent. Even this, however, will mean a bigger mortgage and bigger house for you.

TRAP

Adjustable-rate mortgages, in general and for most people, are traps. They contain numerous pitfalls that the average borrower just isn't aware of. For example, when you get an adjustable rate mortgage with a 5 percent teaser, the "true" rate may be 6 or 7 percent. What does that mean? It means that even if interest rates don't go up within a few adjustment periods you'll be paying at the higher-percent interest rate soon enough. To put it another way, even if rates don't go up, your monthly payments could increase.

TRAP

Another trap has to do with negative amortization. Some of the adjustable loans keep the monthly payments down by adding the interest to the principal. In other words, you end up owing more than you borrowed!

There are other pitfalls with adjustable-rate mortgages and these are covered in Chapter 11, on financing.

Where, Exactly, Should I Look for Financing?

Thus far we've discussed how to qualify for a mortgage and the amount you can get. There remains the question of to whom do you go to get that mortgage. Here are some answers:

Savings and loan associations (thrifts)

Banks

Mortgage bankers (those who fund mortgages themselves)

Mortgage brokers (those who act as retailers for lenders)

Credit unions

Insurance companies (usually accessible through mortgage bankers or brokers)

Corporate financing (through your company)

Letters of credit (from banks or individuals)

Private lenders

Farmers Home Administration

Sources for all the above can be found in the yellow pages of your telephone book. Check under Financing, Mortgages, Home Loans, and related categories.

How Much House Can I Really Afford?

As we've seen, the amount you can afford is pretty much arbitrary. It's a function of your ability to repay. The more you can repay, in terms of the monthly payment you can afford, the more house you can get.

Keep in mind that another function of getting a mortgage is your credit rating or your track history in repaying loans. Here we've assumed right along that it's excellent. If it's not, then you may have to pay a higher interest rate, or you may not get a loan at all. (An exception is an equity loan, for which only the property has to qualify.)

Most people have a ballpark figure in mind when they start house hunting. If you've worked through the sheets provided in this chapter, you should have a much closer idea. Now, get out there and start looking!

6
How to Find the Right House

It isn't like looking for a needle in a haystack. It's more like looking for a piece of hay.

Once you've determined how much of a house you can afford, it's time to start the hunt. You'll want to marshal all the resources at your command to locate the perfect house, particularly since you'll probably have an enormous selection to choose from. However, simply darting about here and there won't do it. You have to set certain parameters. These usually include the following.

Your House-Hunting Parameters

1. How many bedrooms will you need?___________

TIP

Most houses have three or four bedrooms. You'll probably have to pay a premium for five or more bedrooms. Houses with fewer than three bedrooms are often more difficult to resell.

2. How many bathrooms will you need?__________

TRAP

Don't buy a house with only one bathroom. It's very difficult to resell.

3. Do you want a newer house with all the modern goodies such as better insulation, copper plumbing, high-efficiency heating and cooling, heavy-duty electrical systems, and what comes with all that—fewer repairs? Or will you settle for the comforts of an older, established home such as a fully grown garden, larger lot, and developed neighborhood? New? [ ] Old [ ]?
4. Are there any special features that you must have? (These include breakfast nooks, work area in the garage, washer and dryer near the bedroom, home office room(s), skylights, and wood paneling.)__________

TIP

Try to be as flexible as possible. The more you must have, the more it's going to cost you.

5. Is there a better school district you want to be in?__________
6. What about being close to a shopping center?__________
7. If you're going to commute, what is the maximum distance you are willing to drive?__________

TIP

Get a map. Indicate those areas which are within range, those which are too far out. It will help you limit your search area.

8. Do you want a two-story, three-story, split-level, or ranch? Or will you accept any style?__________
9. What about colors? If you can't stand a blue house or a green house or a yellow house, you better recognize this fact up front. Are you willing to repaint?__________
10. Do you want a fireplace? What about a pool? Air conditioning?

TIP

You'll pay substantially more for a pool house. However, a fireplace and even air conditioning (in many areas) are standard equipment these days. Expect to pay less for a house without them.

11. Do you want a big lot? Does it have to have a view? Do you mind being on a busy street? What about a corner lot?__________

TRAP

Big lots are supposed to be better and cost more. But in reality they require much more time, effort, and money to maintain and frequently are harder to resell. A view lot will always cost more, but it will bring more on resale. A corner lot means street noise on two sides and is often objectionable. Being on a busy street makes a house almost twice as hard to resell as does being on a quiet street.

How Do I Get Started?

Okay, you have an idea of what you want and you're ready to look. Where do you begin? Start by listing the number of resources you have for finding just the right house. In most cases they are limited to:

1. Checking the paper
2. Driving around looking for "For Sale" signs
3. Talking and working with agents

4. Checking bulletin boards
5. Talking to friends, acquaintances, and people at work

The important thing here is not to reinvent the wheel. When you begin looking for just the right house, what you're really doing is gathering information. You want to learn which neighborhoods you can afford and in which you feel safe, what those neighborhoods look like, what the traffic and public transportation are like, the quality of schools and shopping, and so forth.

It's a lot of information and you want to get it the quickest and easiest way possible. One way is to go around investigating by yourself. In a few weeks you'll turn up most of the answers.

An easier way is to contact one or two good agents, first. Their business requires gathering this information. They already have it. In the matter of a single conversation, they can impart to you information it would take you weeks to gather on your own. They can also be an excellent source for directing you to others who may have knowledge that they don't possess.

TRAP

Always, always carry a map with you. When a broker says that the Maple Heights and Laurel Park areas are affordable, ask for the price range of those areas and then mark it on your map. You'll be surprised how 10 minutes later you can't remember whether it was Maple Park or Laurel Heights or what. When an agent tells you about schools or malls or public transportation, mark them on the map. Unless you're very familiar with the area, the information will be in one ear and out the other in moments.

How Do I "Sniff" Out the Areas?

Once you get a broker to whittle down the general areas that are in your price range, do some investigation on your own.

First, drive the areas. You should look for how people keep up their properties. Are all the lawns nicely mowed? Or are their broken cars and auto parts strewn across lawns? Watch for broken fences, scattered trash, and graffiti—sure signs the neighborhood is going downhill and may be unsafe.

Check the public transportation. Stop at the bus or train station and talk to people. Find out how long it really takes to commute. If you're going to be driving on a thruway or freeway, wait until rush hour and then drive it yourself. Use a watch to determine just how long it takes you. (You may be surprised!)

Check out public facilities. Look for libraries, fire stations, police departments, and hospitals as well as malls and grocery stores. Are they convenient and well located?

Walk the area. Once you whittle down the areas even more on the basis of items you discovered (above) by driving around, stop, park your car and start walking. Talk to anyone you meet. Ask about problems in the area, about schools, about bad neighbors. When you're doing this, you can also ask if people know of any house not yet listed that might be coming on the market soon. (We'll have more to say about this later.)

TRAP

Don't be the sort of person who shops by car. Probably the biggest mistake that buyers make when checking out an area is not walking it. Nothing substitutes for shank's mare when it comes to discovering the kind of neighborhood you're in.

How Do I Find a Specific House?

By now you should have narrowed down the neighborhoods. You want to live between Ethel Street and Oak Boulevard or in the Pinewood or Horizon Hills or Wildfield tracts. You're ready to find the house. What you need to do is to quickly get a handle on every for-sale house in your price range in those areas.

Isn't that an overwhelming task?

Not really. Be aware that in most areas, 90 percent or more of the homes are listed with agents. The reason is simple: The vast majority of sellers don't have the time, expertise, or energy to sell their property themselves. (Also, it's a fact that buyers rarely purchase a home they "drop into" because of a "For Sale" sign. It's simply too hard to discover all the houses that are for sale in an area. It's much easier to check with someone who can give you a list.)

So, start with the agents. Have an agent show you the listed houses in the area you're considering. We'll go into detail on the best ways to do that in the next chapter.

Should I Check Out the FSBOs?

FSBO is an acronym for "for sale by owner." There are always some FSBOs available in any neighborhood. When the market is hot and houses are selling well, sellers try to avoid paying a commission by selling themselves. When the market is cold and houses aren't selling, sellers eventually give up on agents and try to sell by themselves.

You should just drop in on the FSBOs. (Usually it's best to call first, since many sellers working without agents are wary of strangers.) When you do drop by, almost always you'll be courteously shown around the property. The troubles don't start until you begin asking about price, terms, and financing.

TRAP

Unfortunately, many FSBO sellers have only a vague idea of what the market price for their house should be. Most often they are asking too much. If you suggest this to them, they may be insulted. In addition, very often they have no idea of how to arrange financing for you. You'll have to handle it yourself. Finally, and most importantly, it is very difficult to negotiate terms or price reductions with them because of the one-on-one relationship between you, the buyer, and them. Unless you're well versed in real estate, it's difficult to deal with FSBO sellers.

TIP

One way of handling FSBOs is to work with a "buyer's agent." Prearrange with an agent to help you out. (See the next chapter for how this is done.) When you find an FSBO that you like, the agent will step in and handle the negotiations. For his role, the agent will receive a partial commission, usually paid by the seller. (Or you may pay the agent a flat fee up front, say $500 or $1000. The agent may arrange a partial commission from the seller.) Many more agents these days are willing to work with buyers in this way.

My own experience with FSBOs has not been particularly successful. As a buyer, I have walked the streets stopping at FSBOs and talking to sellers. I have tried to buy the homes for myself. Unless the seller is just trying to sell by owner for a few weeks before listing, the results have almost universally been dismal. Typically a determined FSBO seller wants too much for the property or is inflexible when it comes to the terms. In other words, I can make a better deal on a property that is listed by an agent.

Can I Find Properties Before They Are Listed?

There is another category of property which, though rarer, offers potentially greater financial opportunities to you, the buyer. That is a property which has not yet come onto the market.

Sellers have a world of reasons for selling. Sometimes it is a well thought-out decision determined over a long period of time. In other cases a sudden event such as job change, illness, or death may cause a quick decision to sell.

Regardless of how it happens, there is always a period of time between when sellers make the decision (or are close to making the decision) and when they actually list the property with an agent. I call this the "golden time."

The Golden Time

During the golden time, the sellers are willing to sell, but haven't yet fully committed to an agent or anyone else. If you can come in at that point with a reasonable offer, the sellers are very likely to accept. They will be thinking about all the hassles of selling that you will save them. No agents to deal with. No commission to pay. No time spent showing the property and waiting for buyers. You're a life-saver if you come during that golden period.

Unfortunately, the golden time lasts only a few days to a few weeks. Also unfortunately, it's very hard to learn about sellers who are in that golden time.

Often it's only through friends or acquaintances or associates at work that you learn that Jim is considering selling his home or Mary is planning to list her property. When you learn of this, act immediately. Contact Mary and Jim that very day or evening at the latest. Tell them you are actively looking to buy a home and would very much like to consider theirs. Will they just let you come over and look?

Then go. Chances are the house will be in a terrible location or will be too small or too big or too crazy. But every once in a while, it's just right. When it is, strike a deal right there and then. Presumably by this time you know what houses are going for in the area and you know what a good price is. Come to terms and have your agent or attorney handle the paperwork later.

By getting to a house before it gets listed or goes up for sale, you can often save a lot of money and get superior terms.

Should I Consider a Fixer-Upper?

There are two main reasons buyers look for fixer-uppers (rundown houses that usually sell for less because of their poor condition). The first is as an investment. The idea is that you'll go in, do the fix-up work, and sell for a profit. There's money to be made here.

The second is that a fixer-upper will sell for less in any given neighborhood. Hence, you might be able to get into the neighborhood you want by buying a fixer-upper while otherwise you'd be excluded because of price.

Both reasons are valid. I've bought more fixer-uppers than I'd care to remember, and most of the time I've gotten good prices and made a profit on resale. But not always.

The most common problem with fixer-uppers is that the buyer, particularly the inexperienced buyer, underestimates the costs of repairs.

"I'll Do It Myself!"

The four most insidious words with regard to a fixer-upper are "I'll do it myself!" "I'll fix: the ceiling, the plumbing, the holes in the wall, the torn wiring, the broken sink and toilet, the gutters, the holes in the roof, the cracked foundation, the broken windows, the leaking pool (and pool pump and filter), the doors, the plaster, the...everything!"

The truth is, the most successful buyers of fixer-uppers are those who can, in fact, do it all themselves, saving fortunes on repair costs. Unfortunately, the most unsuccessful are those who realize, usually too late, that they don't have the aptitude, knowledge, or tenacity to do it all themselves. Consider that putting in a water heater (the simplest of fixer-upper jobs) should cost you no more than $150, including the heater and parts. The same job hired out to a plumber will cost upward of $300. Repairing a roof yourself could cost $1000 in shingles or $2500 to hire someone to do it. Installing floor tile could cost $250 in tile and glue or $1000 to hire it out. See the point?

If you are a fixer-upper person, by all means give it a try. But if you don't know the working end of a screwdriver or how to strip wire for a plug, forget it. You don't have a chance. If you have to hire it out, the money you saved on the purchase of a fixer-upper will be spent many times over getting the place fixed up.

To get a better idea of how to handle a fixer-upper, I suggest my 1996 book *Find It, Buy It, Fix It!*

TIP

Try going partners with a renovator when buying a fixer-upper. You'll agree to live in the house for a set period of time, say 2 years. During that time your partner will fix up the place, then you'll sell for a profit that you'll split. The trick is to find a handy person who's looking to make a few bucks on the side fixing up a property. Of course, you'll have to tolerate living in a house that's never quite finished. But your partner may help with the down payment and the monthly payment, and you could end up living in a property you'd never be able to afford by yourself.

TRAP

Be sure you're getting a terrific price when you buy a fixer-upper. In tight markets and in good neighborhoods, rundown houses often go for nearly as much as properties in good condition. That's a ripoff for you, the buyer. When buying a fixer-upper, be prepared to spend no more than 75 percent of the market price of comparable houses. If you spend more, you're not getting a good deal and ultimately you'll probably lose money!

Beware of Overbuilt Homes!

You're looking at a house in a neighborhood that typically has three- and four-bedroom, single-story homes. Suddenly you come across a house with two stories and six bedrooms. The owner has "added on." There's an extra bath, a remodeled kitchen. In fact, the house looks like a palace. And the price is palatial.

Nevertheless, it offers so much that you're thinking of some way that you can get into it. Sell the car, the boat, the dog? Work an extra two jobs? Anything to get this wonderful house.

Forget it. The house is a loser, a white elephant. The only reason it looks so terrific is that it's a BMW surrounded by Fords. Put it with other BMWs and Mercedes and Rolls and it'll look common.

There are a relatively few things that an owner can do to add on to a house and still recoup the money invested. Remodeling a kitchen is one. But start adding floors and rooms and very quickly the house becomes overbuilt—the neighborhood doesn't justify the work that's done.

Typically in such a situation, the owners are asking far less than the actual costs of the remodeling that they spent, but far more than surrounding houses cost. It's going to take them a very long time to find a buyer. And if you're that buyer, it's going to take you a very long time when you want to resell.

TRAP

Buyers (like you) look for location first, the building second. If a house is too big or overbuilt for a location, it becomes a problem. You don't want to purchase someone else's problem.

TIP

Buy the least expensive house in the most expensive neighborhood. If you do, you multiply your chances for making money later on when you resell.

Don't Give Up

As you go from house to house, remember that a big factor is exhaustion. It's not just being physically tired. It's the fact that after a while, all the houses start to look the same. Therefore it's a good idea to keep in mind the following:

1. Always take a notepad and map with you. Mark the location of the house on the map and write down special features on the pad. If the owner offers you a fact sheet, save it even if you don't seem interested in the house at the time. Later on, you may think about it and realize the home had more appeal than you at first realized.

2. Never look at more than three houses in any one session. After that, you're no longer being careful. You're just running through not paying attention to the details that could make you fall in love with a place. If you need to see a lot of houses, take big breaks. See three in the morning, then stop and have lunch. See three more, then stop and do something else. See three more in the evening. Nine houses in one day is the absolute capacity of almost any prospective buyer. Even with nine, the features of one will begin to blend in with the features of another.

3. Try to get a Polaroid or digital camera and snap a picture of the houses that appeal to you. A picture *is* worth 1000 words. You'll instantly remember the features of a house, once you see a picture of the outside or some room inside. Frequently, agents or owners will provide you with photocopied pictures.

4. Sketch floor plans that you like on your notepad. It helps to remember and is also a good means of comparing one house with another.

5. Don't be afraid to ask questions. Many buyers worry that they'll be thought foolish if they ask about drain pipes or washrooms or taxes or something they think everyone else knows about. There are no foolish questions, only foolish buyers who don't ask questions. A seemingly simple questions may open up a whole line of concern that you weren't aware of.

TIP

It's far better to ask about the problems of a house before you buy than to be stuck with them after you own it.

7
How to Pick a Good Agent

Most people think picking real estate agents is like picking apples out of a barrel. There are going to be a few shiny ones here and there, a few bad ones on the bottom, but overall they are going to be pretty much the same. Unfortunately, that's simply not true. Yes, there are always a few bad apples, but the real distinction has to do not so much with ethics as with ability. Some agents are able to help you, but many are not.

It's important to understand what I mean by "ability." I'm not talking about understanding the laws of your state with regard to the licensing of agents or the selling of real estate. Today, in most states agents must pass strict tests as well as continue their education to make sure they understand what their legal and fiduciary responsibilities are. In this sense, the overwhelming number of agents are able. It's when it comes to serving your needs that many fall down.

My father, who was a successful agent for over 30 years, used to say, "When I first got my license, I thought I was ready to sell real estate. It wasn't until 10 years later that I finally learned how to really be an agent."

To understand what he meant, it's important to realize just what's involved in being a real estate agent. Once you see the selling of property from the agent's perspective, you'll get a whole new view of how to pick the right agent.

What Does It Really Mean to Be a Real Estate Agent?

According to Hollywood, the real estate agent drives a Mercedes or at worst a Caddy or BMW. He or she (most agents are women) meets clients over cocktails, attends flashy parties with lenders, and makes oodles of money (certainly into the six figures).

The truth is somewhat less exciting. According to several surveys, the average agent in 1994 made under $30,000 a year. In addition, out of that $30,000 the agent paid for:

A business automobile

Gas and maintenance for that car

Phone

Dress clothes for work

Other expenses involved in operating a business

In other words, after expenses, the average real estate agent was pretty close to the poverty line in terms of income *from real estate!*

"How can that be?" I'm sure you're asking. The agents you've met always seemed so successful.

The truth? It's mostly a front. A lot of agents simply work hard at looking good.

You also have to understand that real estate is actually a second or part-time career for many individuals. It attracts an enormous number of people who are looking for less than full-time work. Typically these are people who have retired from another profession (teaching, the military, government, or large corporations) and are now on a pension and looking to pick up a few extra bucks. Often these people have dabbled a little in real estate and are in an office as much to look for bargains for themselves as to service you or other clients. In the trade these people are called "inactive" agents.

The real trouble is that because inactive agents often have another steady source of income, they aren't "hungry" enough to get out there, find the really good houses, and negotiate the toughest deals. (After all, whether they make a sale or not they know they'll survive—because of their pension.)

How many "inactive" agents are out there? The easiest way to tell is to remember the 80/20 rule. Every active real estate broker (and I was one for many years) knows that 20 percent of the agents sell

80 percent of the property. The corollary is that 80 percent of the agents are only selling 20 percent of the property. That big 80 percent represents the "inactive" group.

TIP

During the real estate recession between 1990 and 1995 a great many of the part-time as well as the "lower 20 percent" agents left the business. In California, for example, during that time period nearly one-third of all agents quit. The result is that those who are left are the more competent agents.

Who Are the Hot 20 Percent?

Let's talk about that 20 percent that's making the vast majority of deals. These are the "active" agents. Typically they are aggressive, often relatively young, individuals who have no means of support other than real estate. To put it bluntly, if they don't make deals, they don't eat.

If you were to isolate this group of individuals, you would find that they typically make over $75,000 a year and probably half make well into six figures. They are out there beating the bushes from dawn till dusk. They look at *every* new house that comes on the market in their area. They are constantly "farming" (talking with potential sellers) to get listings. When they get an offer, they go in there and negotiate all night if necessary to get the seller to either accept or compromise.

Is this the agent you want working for you? You bet it is!

How Do I Separate the Active from the Inactive Agents?

Okay, you want an active agent. How do you get one?

First off, remember that active agents are *active*. They should:

1. Have a number of properties listed
2. Be always working tirelessly evenings and weekends
3. Be extremely familiar with the market in your area

4. Be ready and able to show you numerous sales they've made *in the past few months*
5. Be busy with real estate (but not too busy to show you houses)

TIP

A recommendation from a friend is a good method of finding the active agent. If your friend has had a positive experience with an agent, it's a good sign. But remember, it's not a guarantee. Your friend might have just been lucky and fallen into the perfect house. The agent's efforts could have been incidental. Even with a recommendation, you need to be sure you've got an active agent.

Are There Active Versus Inactive Offices?

Just as there are two types of agents, there are also two types of offices: the active office where sales are constantly happening, and the inactive office where the agents sit around and commiserate with one another about the slow (to them) real estate market.

There are a few good ways to tell the two types of offices apart:

1. An active office almost always advertises heavily. Check the ads in your local paper.
2. An active office usually has quite a few agents and they always seem to be scurrying around, not sitting at their desks drinking coffee and reading the newspaper.
3. An active office usually has promotions going on to induce greater activity from agents. Walking in, you will often see "salesperson of the month" and "lister of the month" awards—TVs or trips to Hawaii for the best producers of the season.
4. Other agents will know of the active offices and often will speak of them grudgingly as people who are always getting the deals done.
5. This is just a personal observation, but I have found that active offices usually have a secretarial staff. The agents are out there

selling, the staff handles the paperwork. In an inactive office (without many sales or much revenue), it seems the agents are stuck with all the secretarial duties.

Just keep in mind that the 80/20 rule still applies even in an active office. It's just that in an inactive office, the hot 20 percent aren't there.

How Do I Find an Active Agent in an Active Office?

If you walk off the street and into an active real estate office (see above), chances are actually against your getting an active agent. The reason is that all agents pull "floor time." This is time they are allowed to sit in the office and pick up potential clients who come in across the transom. You walk in and you get the current floor agent or, if there's a receptionist, the next agent who is "up."

You'll immediately know this person. How? While other people in the office smile at you, this agent will quickly come up, introduce himself, and ask how he can be helpful.

Since almost all agents, active or inactive, are people-oriented, they almost certainly will be polite, charming, and apparently helpful. But if they are inactive agents, they are wasting your time.

TIP

When you walk into a real estate office cold, don't accept the first agent who comes to see you. Rather, say that you are waiting to see someone, an agent, but you can't remember the name. Now, while the receptionist or the floor agent begins listing the names of the agents in the company, look around the walls of the reception area. As noted, a great many active companies will have "agent of the month" awards hanging there. Very frequently, the award for the past 10 or 12 months will have gone repeatedly to one agent. Just point to the plaque and say, "That's her." Or "That's him." You'll be quickly introduced to the most active agent in the office.

If there are no awards to tip you off, then ask to see the broker. It's important to understand that all real estate offices are organized around one person, the broker. Everyone else is an associate agent. (Even other brokers may have their licenses subordinated to the main broker.)

In a small office, the broker acts as a salesperson. In a larger office, however, the broker typically sits somewhere in a back office and handles closings and other difficult work. In a very large office, the broker frequently may be out making big deals while subordinate brokers handle the day-to-day work.

When you request the broker by name, you are usually asked in response, "Will your name be recognized by our broker?" In other words, do you have an appointment?

Just reply, "My business concerns one of your agents. I want to speak only to the broker."

Just the hint that there could be some problem will get you an audience. Real estate companies dread complaints or angry clients. Most will bend over backward to avoid any kind of dissatisfaction.

When you are ushered in to see the broker (or the person who is in charge at the moment in the case of a very large office), carefully explain that you have not yet talked to any agent in the office (thereby avoiding the problem of having one agent or another "claim" you as a client). Tell the broker you are going to be buying a house in the very near future and you want to deal with the most active agent in the office in terms of sales. No one else will do.

The broker may chuckle inwardly at your boldness, but in most cases will tell you who that agent is. And you're on your way. (If the broker refuses, leave. There are almost as many real estate companies to choose from as there are houses for sale!)

Should I Aim for a Large "Franchise" Real Estate Company?

Don't be misled into picking your agent on the basis of the real estate company's name recognition. Over the past few decades, franchising has proliferated the real estate market. But a real estate franchise is no better or worse than a fast-food franchise such as McDonald's or Burger King. All that you are assured of in a fast-food franchise is that you will get no less than a certain standard quality of hamburger and service. The same holds true for real estate franchises.

In nearly every state, each real estate office, regardless of the franchise name, is individually owned and operated. What you're dealing with is the local broker and agents who have adopted the sign, the coat, and the procedures of a franchising company. However, you still go out with your individual agent to see properties, and it's your agent with whom you'll consult when making an offer.

The franchise office is no better or worse than a nonfranchised office in providing you with good, active agents—it just has name recognition, more advertising clout, and sometimes nicer jackets. Agent for agent, I don't feel there's a significant difference. (Some franchises offer their own financing and escrows, which can be a convenience. But in my opinion, it's always better to get your own financing and use an independent escrow.)

On the other hand, if something should go wrong, sometimes it's easier (sometimes harder!) to deal with a franchise company. At least here you know there's a big corporate entity that is concerned with keeping its good name and its customers happy.

It's important to remember that real estate, almost more than any other business, is highly personalized. The deal you get will depend mostly on the one person with whom you deal. You can get a great active agent with a nonfranchised company just as well as with a franchised one.

How Do I Help an Agent Help Me?

Once you find an active agent, you must decide whether he or she is right for you. Watch for obvious problems such as personality clashes or basic differences in outlook. In addition, you want to be sure that the agent isn't so aggressive as to overwhelm you. You want to be able to control your agent, not the other way around. Remember agents influence your decision by what they do or do not say. Be sure that they aren't using this power to manipulate you into something you may not want.

You will want to be forthright with an agent. Let the agent know your price range (see Chapter 5 for clues on how much you can afford). Tell the agent the areas you want to locate in. The agent isn't a mind reader and can't find the perfect house for you until you give the agent the parameters of what you're looking for. This doesn't mean you need to tell agents everything about your finances or your intentions, as we'll see shortly. Just offer enough to enable them to work for you.

TIP

It's okay to work with several agents, but only one at a time. If you are going to be looking at property on a weekend, work with only one agent for that weekend. Don't hip-hop from one to the next. Only when your relationship peters out and the agent stops showing you properties you want to see should you move on. Reward a good agent with your loyalty, and the agent will reward you with good work.

When you find that your current agent is no longer productive, try another. But be "up front" with both agents. Tell the second agent the properties you've already seen. Ask the second agent for something new or different to show you.

There is a good reason for working with more than one agent. First, while the vast majority of properties listed by agents are put on the Multiple Listing Service (MLS), where nearly all agents can work on them, some agents keep really good properties as "pocket listings." Other agents won't know about them and, therefore, won't show you the properties. Further, in some areas, groups of agents have banded together to form competing listing systems. One agent may not be able to show you all the properties that are listed.

On the other hand, understand that the agent who first shows you the property you eventually buy may be entitled to a portion of the commission even if a different agent eventually makes the sale. This could cause hard feelings or even problems later on should a different agent submit the offer. Instead of working hard to negotiate the best price and terms for you, the various agents could get into a squabble over who gets what portion of the commission.

Work with only one agent at a time and tell that agent the properties you've already seen and who else you've worked with. It will save you time and possible problems later on.

TRAP

Years ago (before the consumer protection movement was even dreamed of) I knew an agent who had a very aggressive style. He would get his clients in his car, which was connected to his office by two-way radio.

(This was before cellular phones.) He would then take them out looking at properties. After he had exhausted his immediate list of properties, he would call his office and ask his secretary to look up other properties to show. Some clients were impressed. They would continue to look until they were exhausted and then ask to be taken back to the office, where their car was located. The agent would refuse! Oh, he wouldn't exactly say, "No!" Instead, he'd tell them about some other house that was just around the corner and was just right for them. He literally kept them prisoner in his car until they finally agreed to make an offer! Of course, they could have always made him stop and then gotten out. But more often than not, the clients were new to the area and had no idea where they were. While some clients did get angry and refuse to consider anything until the agent brought them back, a surprising number actually were coerced into making offers! Fortunately, such actions today are unheard of. But the story illustrates an important point. Some agents are more actively aggressive than you want or can handle. If that's the case—run, don't walk, away. They'll coerce you into bad deals every time.

The Agent's Responsibility Is Not Always to You!

This is a most important point that most buyers simply don't understand. Let's say that you've found an active agent whom you like and with whom you can work. You must now come to grips with the fact that, in most cases, this agent *does not work for you!* He or she is the agent of and works for the seller.

It doesn't matter that your agent shows you around to many houses listed by other agents on the Multiple Listing Service. It doesn't matter that the house you decide to make an offer on has a separate agent who listed it. (This can be confusing to buyers, particularly when very often there is one agent—yours—who shows you a house and takes your offer and another agent—the one who listed the property—who seems to represent the seller.) Usually the agent who shows you around is the "subagent" of the agent who listed the property. In other words, *both* are very often the agents of the seller!

TIP

The law of agency in all states is quite clear. It requires that an agent maintain a *fiduciary* relationship with whomever that agent represents. Usually that's the seller.

If the "subagent" who's been showing you around takes an offer from you and presents it to a seller, who is represented by a listing agent, both of these people may have a fiduciary relationship, not with you, but with the seller.

What does having a fiduciary relationship mean? It means that the agents owe the seller "integrity, honesty, and loyalty." That translates into the following.

1. Unless the seller has authorized it, your seller's agent can't disclose how much less than the selling price the seller might take, even if the agent knows of a specific figure! (This isn't to say that many agents don't hint at the lower figure, but they aren't supposed to come right out and tell you, for example, that the seller said, "My price is $100,000, but I'm so desperate to sell I'd take $75,000, *but don't you dare tell that to any buyer!*")

2. The agent can't disclose that the seller might accept terms more favorable to you unless the seller has authorized the agent to tell you.

3. On the other hand, if you tell the agent that you're desperate to buy, that even though you're offering $75,000 you'd be willing to pay $80,000, the agent is *obligated* to tell the seller what you said! (Working with a seller's agent is almost like having an enemy spy in your camp!)

Of course, in actual practice there is some bending of the rules. And a good agent will always attempt to work fairly with both buyer and seller.

Nevertheless, in today's world, where consumers are so litigious, many agents are hesitant to do anything which a seller might construe as violating the fiduciary relationship and which might result in a lawsuit against them. Hence, when you work with a seller's agent (or subagent), don't expect advice on how to get the best terms or price.

TIP

When you're working with a seller's agent, even one you consider on your side, button you lips. Don't tell the seller's agent the highest you'll go on an offer. Don't let the agent know the best terms you'll give the seller. Think of the agent as the seller's earphone. Don't whisper anything in that you don't want the seller to hear. Keep your own confidences.

Are There Agents Who Work for *Both* Buyer and Seller?

There is no easy solution to the problem of agency for buyers. One answer, however, that is gaining increasing popularity in some areas of the country is to have a "dual agent."

A dual agent represents both buyer and seller. This agent owes both the sellers and you "integrity, honesty, and loyalty." However, the dual agent still *may not tell you if the seller will accept a price less than the property is listed for.* However, to compensate for this, the dual agent may also not tell the seller that you'd be willing to pay more than the price you offer. (The same generally holds true with terms.)

Thus, while the dual agent really isn't 100 percent on your side, the agent also isn't 100 percent on the seller's side either.

TRAP

Don't assume that just because your agent isn't the lister of the property he or she is a "dual" agent. Unless your agent specifies whom he or she is working for, you can probably assume it's the seller.

How Do I Know Whom My Agent Is Working For?

Ask.

Your agent is obligated to tell you. Further, before you sign any documents, including a sales offer, your agent should present you with a written statement describing who that agent works for (seller, dual, or buyer). Many states now require a formal disclosure as part of their agency law. (California, for example, requires dual agents to give a signed statement to that effect to both buyer and seller.)

TIP

An agent cannot generally perform as a dual agent without the express written consent of *both* buyer and seller. Absent that express written consent, the presumption is usually that the agent represents the seller.

Should I Work with a "Buyer's Agent"?

As if it isn't confusing enough already, there is yet another designation of agent we've hinted at, a "buyer's agent." This is an agent who truly works for you, the buyer. (After all, if sellers can have their agents, why can't buyers?)

There's no reason not to work with a buyer's agent and several good reasons to do so. After all, it's the only way you can be sure the agent is on your side. Remember, a true buyer's agent has a fiduciary responsibility to you, not to the seller. Such agents must tell you everything they know about the property and about the seller that's to your advantage, including any information about the seller's willingness to accept a lower price or better terms.

The only problem in dealing with a buyer's agent usually is the fee. If you want a buyer's agent, you sometimes may have to pay the commission yourself!

At this point I'm sure some buyers are ready to hurl this book out the window. Pay a commission when you buy?! In addition to the cost of the house, the down payment, the closing costs, and on and on. Add to that the cost of a buyer's agent's commission? That's crazy!

Not really, and in most cases the seller ends up paying for the buyer's agent anyhow. Buyer's agents are adept at working out the commission with the sellers. The buyer's agent's fee is usually half of a full commission. (If the commission rate in your area is 6 percent, the buyer's agent's commission may be only 3 percent.) Often a deal is worked out in which the seller agrees to pay your agent half the commission and the seller's agent the other half. Thus, it may not cost you any more than if you had worked with a seller's or a dual agent. On the other hand, by working with a buyer's agent, you might save so much on the purchase price that it would be worth your while to pay a commission yourself!

TIP

Some areas of the country have many buyer's agents; other areas have almost none. They do advertise in phone books and in newspapers. In addition, regular seller's agents in almost every area know of buyer's agents and usually are willing to at least let you know who they are, if not recommend them to you, once you make it plain that's what you want.

Should you use a buyer's agent?

The vast majority of buyers don't and that's unfortunate. The only way to get an agent really on your side is to use a buyer's agent. I wholeheartedly suggest you look for one when you get ready to buy.

What About the Bad Apples?

As noted earlier, there are always a few bad apples. These are agents who either are outright crooks or are so unaware of real estate laws that they can cause you harm in a deal. How do you avoid these?

Fortunately, in most cases the bad apples don't last long. After a few deals they often mess up so badly that there are letters of complaint to the state real estate regulatory body, which either revokes their license or disciplines them. The danger is that you might run into one of these bad apples before they get thrown out. How do you protect yourself?

I wish I had a surefire answer. However, the tips here are the same ones that are given when picking any person whom you give your confidence to when it comes to your finances:

1. Find out how long the agents have been in the business. Even if the salesperson has been in business only a few years, the office should have been around a long time. Do business only with a

agent or office who has a long track record—5 to 7 years at the least.

2. Work with a national franchisee. While earlier I stressed that this is no guarantee you'll get an active agent, it does give you some assurance of at least minimal quality in terms of procedures. Besides, if the agent should be truly incompetent and negligent, you can always appeal to the national office of the chain.

3. Ask to see the agent's real estate license. In all states, agents *must be licensed* and that license must be prominently displayed in their office. They'll be pleased to show it to you.

In truth, most buyers are going to consider only the above three suggestions (plus recommendations of friends). However, if you're really concerned, here are some additional steps you can take to find out about an agent's background:

4. Check with the local better business bureau or (in an extreme case) the local district attorney's office to see if there are now pending or have ever been any complaints against the agent or the office.

5. Call the state real estate department and ask if the agent's license has ever been revoked or suspended or if the agent has ever been disciplined. (This is public information to which you are entitled.)

Quite frankly, few buyers will ever take these steps. In most cases, we tend to accept a friendly smile and a solid handshake as evidence of competence and honesty. And in most cases things work out just fine. Remember, however, we are now considering those very few bad apples.

TRAP

The worst thing that you can do is to find out you've been dealing with a bad agent after something has happened—after you've made an offer that has somehow gone awry and has resulted in a money loss to you or the threat of a lawsuit from the seller or some other injured party. A few calls may suddenly tell you that this agent has been in hot water since she got her license.

> Then you'll say to yourself, "If only I had investigated first!" Remember, it takes only one or two phone calls and perhaps 15 minutes of time talking to the right people to get a minimal background check on the person who is going to advise you on what is probably the biggest investment you'll make in your life.

Unfortunately, the truth is that you can seldom be completely sure about an agent (or other person with whom you deal financially). I recently learned of a very unusual case, an agent who was falsifying loan documents. This person was telling buyers they could obtain financing that they obviously could not qualify for, and was getting it! We'll call him Jim (obviously not his real name). Jim was securing false verifications of employment (which your employer fills out, giving your salary) and false verifications of deposit (which a bank or an S&L fills out, giving the cash on hand that you have for a down payment). Both these verifications are what a lender bases a loan on. Since most loans today are sold in the secondary market to government agencies, to falsify them is a federal offense investigated by the Federal Bureau of Investigation or the Treasury Department. Fraud here is a serious offense.

Jim was blandly falsifying these documents for buyers, telling them not to worry; it was done every day, it was just a formality, and they'd never have anything to worry about. The interesting thing is that Jim had been falsifying documents successfully for over 7 years! He was considered one of the most successful members of the real estate profession, a pillar of the community.

Perhaps he might have gone on another 7 years, but circumstances eventually did him in. As it turned out he was doing more and more deals with more and more people who couldn't really qualify for mortgages, and the lenders never suspected fraud until there was a downturn in the economy. Since in Jim's case the vast majority of mortgages he was placing involved people who were just marginally able to handle the payments, when things got rough and the borrowers lost their jobs, they couldn't pay and stopped. Many of their mortgages went into foreclosure.

One day, a secretary for one of the secondary lenders was going through paperwork and happened to notice that a lot of foreclosures in the area involved borrowers who had originally purchased homes through Jim. An investigation was quietly launched. It was a simple matter to go back several years and check on the verifications of deposit with banks and S&Ls and the verifications of employment with employers. It quickly became clear that outright fraud had been committed.

As a result, Jim had his real estate business shut down. Even worse, the buyers were likewise charged with fraud. That meant that they were personally subject to any losses that the lenders incurred in the foreclosures as well as subject to civil and criminal penalties!

The moral of this story is that even a bad apple once in a great while can appear to be a shiny, bright apple. Of course, as P. T. Barnum and W. C. Fields were heard to say, "You can never cheat an honest man." If those buyers had really thought it through, they would never have allowed Jim to falsify their verifications.

Picking the right agent is certainly the second most important decision you'll make—after picking the right house. Take the time to make it wisely.

8
How Do You Buy a Home?

Imagine trying to win a game of football without knowing the rules. You'd send your team out into the field not knowing the difference between quarters or innings. How many points would you get for a touchdown or a field goal? It wouldn't matter how professional your team was. If you didn't know how the game was played, even a grammar school team could beat you.

Real estate is much the same way. Buying a home is not like buying anything else. It's not like buying a car, or a computer, or a jar of mayonnaise. It has its own rules and its own procedures which, in most cases, are rigorously followed.

If you've bought a home before, you probably have an idea of how it's done. But if it's been some time since you bought, or if this is going to be your first purchase, the process may seem mysterious, even arcane.

We're going to change all that in this chapter. We're going to look at the process of buying a home, giving some tips and revealing some traps as we go.

The 12 Steps in Making a Purchase

1. You decide you want to buy (or at least want to look).
2. Along the way you talk with one or more agents.

3. You find the home of your dreams (you hope!) and make a *written* offer on a document called a purchase or sales agreement, usually for less than the sellers are asking. (Verbal offers aren't illegal, just unenforceable.)
4. If the sellers don't accept, they may make a counteroffer, which you may in turn decline and then counter.
5. The sellers eventually accept your offer, or one of your counters. (If the sellers don't accept, start over with Step 1.)
6. Your agent or you open *escrow*. Used today in most states, it is a licensed and bonded company which acts as a neutral third party. The escrow receives all funds, makes sure that all documents are properly executed, and when all the conditions of the sales agreement (and the lender) have been met, transfers title to you, records the mortgage in favor of the lender, and gives the sellers their fund. Escrow typically lasts 45 to 60 days.
7. You secure your financing (if you haven't already).
8. You fulfill any other obligations you're committed to as part of the sales agreement, such as putting extra cash into the deposit and approving a contingency. The sellers do likewise, such as providing a termite clearance, obtaining clear title, and clearing any contingencies they may have.
9. Your lender agrees to fund your mortgage.
10. You have a final "walk-through" inspection of the property.
11. You sign the final documents; the escrow records the documents and transfers the funds.
12. You get possession and the key.

What Am I Signing in the Sales Agreement?

The key to the whole process is the sales agreement. We've already covered some of the basics, such as finding a house and working with an agent, and we'll cover closings in Chapter 12. So let's move right up to the big document that handles the sale. The sales agreement, also called the purchase agreement and sometimes the deposit receipt, is the document you use to make an offer on the property. Once your offer is accepted, it becomes the agreement for the sale.

In the old days in real estate the sales agreement was usually just one page long. It had very little printed material and was composed mostly of empty spaces that the agent filled in. That has changed dramatically.

Over the years dissatisfied buyers and sellers (a very small minority, but with important implications) have gone to court, fighting over various issues such as specific performance or deposits or damages. What was discovered was that very frequently the sales agreement, drawn up not by an attorney but by a real estate agent, did not hold up. Suits were lost because the agreement was defective. This resulted in additional suits against agents, almost all of whom now carry a form of malpractice or errors and omissions insurance.

It also resulted in a new kind of sales agreement. The new agreement is frequently six pages or longer. Almost all of it is printed out—the agent typically only checks boxes or fills in dollar amounts.

In fact, there are very few places that the agent even has the opportunity to write anything out. The whole emphasis is on seeing to it that relatively few terms can be added for fear that they may void or weaken the agreement.

About the only place that the agent can add anything is in the realm of contingency clauses, as explained in Chapter 9. Usually there are only a few lines left for such additions near the end of the document.

A sales agreement is a legally binding document. Once the seller signs it, it binds both the buyer (you) and the seller to its terms regarding the sale of the property.

TIP

Because the sales agreement is a legal document, you are encouraged to have your real estate attorney explain the full ramifications of it to you before you fill it out.

In addition to legal considerations, there are several important practical issues, which we turn to next. A typical real estate sales agreement includes language covering the following areas. If it does not cover these areas, you should ask your agent or attorney why it doesn't.

What's in a Typical Sales Agreement

1. Price, down payment, and deposit
2. Specific terms for all financing
3. Street improvements or bonds—if any, who pays for them
4. When you will be given occupancy (discussed below)
5. The term of the escrow (how long it will be open)
6. How you will take title (tenants in common, joint tenancy, community property, and so on; see your lawyer, since there are important tax and legal ramifications for how you take title)
7. Liquidated damages (discussed in Chapter 9)
8. Arbitration in case of disputes (discussed shortly)
9. Who will hold the keys and when they will be turned over to you (normally when you take possession at the close of escrow)
10. Any personal property involved (discussed shortly)
11. Foreign tax withholding (applies only if the seller is a foreigner)
12. Seller's statement of the condition of the property
13. Seller's warranties
14. Physical inspection (discussed below)
15. Termite report (required by most lenders; if the lender doesn't require it, you should)
16. Soil or geological tests (found in areas with earthquakes or other soil problems)
17. Flood or water hazards (noting if the property is in any flood hazard area)
18. Zoning problems (indicating if the property is in a special zone, such as a "coastal zone," which could affect your ability to build or add on)
19. Home protection plan (which pays for damage or problems with the heating, plumbing, electrical, and other systems, as discussed below)
20. Energy retrofit requirements (local or state ordinances requiring additional insulation to be placed in the house when the property is sold)
21. How prorations will be handled (discussed later)

Many of the areas covered by the sales agreement, such as price, are obvious. Others are discussed in different sections of this book. Below, however, we're going to look at some selected areas of a typical sales agreement that are of particular interest to most buyers because they reflect on the purchase process.

What Is Important About Occupancy? (#4)

The question here is: When will you take possession of the property? The most common answer is at the close of escrow after title has been recorded in your name.

The danger with occupancy is that the sellers won't move out. There are many reasons the sellers might not move. A new house they are planning to move into might not be ready. Or there might be illness in the family and a family member might not be easily moved. Or they could just be ornery.

Whatever the reason, if they don't move, it spells trouble for you. If the sellers are still in possession of the house once you get title, you can't easily have them removed. (In the old days "self-help eviction" was allowed—you could physically go in and throw them out! That's been a taboo for quite a few years now.)

To get the sellers out you might need to conduct an "unlawful detainer" action through the courts. This usually takes about a month, may cost upward of $1000, and usually requires the services of an attorney.

TIP

There's an easy way to ensure that there is no problem with occupancy. It involves two steps.

Step 1: Most sales agreements state when occupancy is to be given. Be sure yours says that the sellers are to be out at least 1 day before the close of escrow.

Step 2: In order to close escrow, you normally have to sign a whole series of documents as well as deposit the down payment into escrow. There are loan agreements for the lender as well as other papers. These may be signed and the down payment deposited as close as 1 day before escrow is set to terminate.

Quite simply, if it were me, I'd refuse to sign until I was convinced that the sellers had completely moved from the property. (If the sellers aren't gone, or close to it, 1 day before the close of escrow—and the transfer of title to you—it isn't likely they'll be gone the next day.)

Be sure your refusal to complete escrow is understood by the agents and the sellers. You have deposited the down payment money into escrow, you are ready, willing, and able to sign. But you won't until the sellers move. If there is a clause in the contract that specifies that the sellers are to be out 1 day before the close of escrow, you should be on steady ground.

It may seem a harsh thing to do and may result in some temporarily hurt feelings, but you'll save yourself an incredible hassle which could result if you take title with the sellers still in possession of the property.

Should I Insist on a Final Inspection? (#14)

Home inspection has become commonplace across the country. You see the property before you make the offer. Then there's a wait of up to several months while financing is arranged, title is cleared, and so forth. How do you know that the property is the same way as when you first saw it? How do you know the seller hasn't smashed holes in the walls and broken the appliances? (Unlikely, but it does happen.)

You know by insisting on a final inspection (also sometimes called a final "walk-through.") Before the deal closes you once again examine what you are buying to be sure it's as you first saw it (or reasonably close).

It's important to remember that a final inspection is not supposed to be an opportunity for you to reconsider your purchase. It is just supposed to be a chance for you to examine the property to see that it's as it was when you made your offer.

TIP

Nonetheless, buyers have used faults found on the final inspection to attempt to back out of a deal at the last minute. To do so, however, there must be a clause in the sales agreement stating that the deal is contingent upon the buyer's approval of the final inspection and, generally, there must actually be something of consequence that is wrong.

Sometimes agents will suggest that a specific date for the final walk-through be written into the sales agreement. This is usually a bad idea. You don't want a specific set date because you don't know when escrow will close and you'll get occupancy. The final inspection should be 1 to 3 days before escrow closes (the day before, if possible).

Also, if you inspect the property too early, the sellers may still be living in it and furniture and carpets not yet removed may conceal potential damage. Try to be sure the sellers are out before you have your final inspection. (This helps solve the problem of occupancy noted above.)

TIP

Be sure the gas, electricity, and water are on when you have your inspection. Otherwise, you won't be able to tell if any of the house's systems are broken.

TRAP

Don't expect the property to look as clean as it did when you first saw it. If the seller was living in the property when you first saw it, carpets and furniture will hide a lot of marks and scuffing. Once the furniture and carpeting are removed these stand out like sore thumbs. Dark scratch marks on walls and scrapes on floors are common. Indentations in carpeting where heavy furniture stood are also common, as is some slight discoloration. (Most of this carpet indentation will disappear within a few days on its own.)

There's very little you can complain about when it comes to normal wear and tear, unless one of the contingencies of your sales agreement was that the seller would repaint and clean the carpets (something to consider).

What you need to look for is any major damage that was not there before and *that the seller did not disclose in the sales agreement or accompanying documents.* What specifically should you look for? Consider this list:

Holes in wall

Broken plaster

Broken windows

Inoperative or broken appliances such as stove, garbage disposal, and oven

Faulty or broken water heater ($300 to repair), as demonstrated by no hot water; gas heater (upward of $1200 to repair); or air conditioner ($1000 or more to repair), as demonstrated by no heat or cooling

Gashes, slashes, or marks in wood floors which will require sanding and revarnishing

Damaged or inoperative light fixtures

Broken or inoperative heating or air-conditioning thermostat (upward of $150 to fix)

Leaky plumbing, as evidenced by new water marks or water on floors

Faults in the electrical system, as evidenced by light switches or wall plugs that don't work

New damage to carpet, such as dirt or, most important, cat or dog urination. I've seen sellers who let their pets run loose in the house after the sales agreement was signed, figuring that it wasn't their problem any more. But if you accept a carpet that has been ruined by urination, it's a big problem for you. Odor is usually the giveaway. If you suspect a problem, don't hesitate to get down on your hands and knees to check it out. Better to discover it now than when you're the owner.

TRAP

Urination from pets *cannot* be effectively removed from carpeting. The carpeting and usually the pad underneath (and sometimes even the flooring!) must be replaced. Sometimes an entire house's carpeting must be replaced to match a small area of damage.

TIP

Don't take the house if there's a carpet problem. Insist it be fixed first, even if that requires the sellers to recarpet the entire house. (Be sure you approve the quality of carpeting and padding they use.)

Should I Get a Professional Inspection?

The answer is simply, yes. There's an entire chapter devoted to what you should look for (Chapter 13). Just remember that in most cases, the seller pays for the inspection, so it won't cost you much, but could save you plenty.

Should I Insist on a Home Protection Plan? (#19)

Several national and a few local companies offer plans which give you some protection for the major systems of your home. Typically they cover plumbing (including water heater), heating, air conditioning, electrical, appliances, and so forth. The idea is that for a set period of time after you move in (usually 1 year), should there be a problem, the home protection company will cover it. The cost is usually nominal, a few hundred dollars for a year's worth of coverage. And most plans are renewable.

TRAP

In order for most home protection plans to be effective, the seller must warrant that all systems are operating and in good condition at the time of the sale. Thus, you want to be sure that the home protection plan is included as part of the sales agreement, that it is purchased at the time of sale, and that the seller gives the appropriate warranties. If you wait until after title transfers, you either may not be able to get the plan or may find that you have to warrant the condition of the various home systems only to discover that some aren't working!

When these plans first came out, I felt they were a waste of money. If the plan cost $400 and you kept it in force for 5 years, it would cost you $2000. In addition, each time you used it there was typically a fairly high deductible, between $30 and $50. I felt that for far less than $2000 over 5 years, you could cover the cost of whatever was likely to go wrong.

In addition, the primary reason these plans originally gained popularity was that real estate agents used them to protect themselves. It was becoming a too common tale that a house would be sold, the water heater would go out, and the buyer would threaten to take the seller and agent to court.

Sellers typically would say, "Drop dead!" to the buyer, and to avoid litigation and hard feelings the agent would end up paying for the water heater replacement. With home protection plans, the cost was covered and the agent would not be bothered. Thus, as noted, I originally felt that they were a waste of money for the buyer.

However, since then the price of everything has skyrocketed, particularly on older homes. I recently had to replace a furnace in a rental that was not covered by a home protection plan (I had owned it for many years). A new furnace, which 10 years ago might have cost $250, today costs $1500.

The same is true for everything else in a home. Thus, particularly if the home is over 7 years old, a home protection plan may be an excellent idea. Just insist that the seller pay for the first year's coverage. (Either party can pay and there's no reason you should, since during the first year it's actually protecting the seller's warranty of the property.)

Should I Agree to an Arbitration Clause? (#7)

Some sales agreements contain arbitration clauses. Typically these refer only to the deposit, but in some cases they may refer to other areas. Basically what they say is that if there is a disagreement, you will submit it to binding arbitration—you will go along with whatever an arbitrator says.

TRAP

You could be giving up significant rights if you sign an arbitration agreement. You could lose the option of suing the seller for damages or even specific performance. On the other hand, the seller could be giving up the same rights, meaning that you could be avoiding the risk of being sued.

If you agree to arbitration, just remember that for it to be effective both you (the buyer) and the seller have to agree. If just one agrees, it won't work. Check with your attorney here.

TIP

Be sure that you know who the arbitrator will be. Many arbitration clauses specify that the arbitrator will be a member of the American Arbitration Association (local members are listed in the yellow pages of your phone book). This is fine, since such members are skilled at arbitration. But they are also quite expensive. It really doesn't make much sense to use an arbitrator when his or her fee may exceed the worth of the item being arbitrated.

What Are Prorations? (#8)

Typically there are always some items that are "prorated." This simply means that items such as taxes, fire insurance, and impounds (see below) are adjusted in proportion to your use.

For example, a fire insurance policy is typically written and paid for 3 years in advance. However, the house may be sold after the policy has been in effect for only 1 year. You, the buyer, are taking over the policy. In this case the seller may want to "prorate" the cost of the insurance policy. In other words, you would pay the seller back for the 2 years you are going to be using the policy.

The same applies to prepaid taxes or taxes that are owing. Adjustments are made in your favor or the seller's favor, depending on when payment was made and what the date of proration is.

There are only two questions with regard to proration: what will be prorated and on what date. Typically all items that are affected by time are prorated. Normally the proration date is the close of escrow.

TIP

You can make proration a contingency on the sale of the property. For example, property taxes may be due in full by March 15 and payable through July 1. You buy on April 1; thus, in theory, you owe the seller for 3 month's of prepaid property taxes. But you insert a contingency clause that insists there is to be no proration of taxes. The seller is desperate to sell and so agrees. You've gained 3 months' worth of taxes.

Making prorations a contingency is most often seen when there are "impound accounts" as part of a mortgage. With an impound account, the lender collects one-twelfth of the annual taxes and fire insurance on the property each month as part of the monthly loan payment. Since payments for taxes and insurance are made for these either annually or semiannually, such funds can add up to a substantial amount. When a buyer assumes (takes over responsibility for repaying) a loan, typically the buyer owes the seller a prorated portion of the impound accounts.

However, many buyers insist that the impound accounts be transferred to them with no prorations. If it's a hot market with lots of buyers, the seller will haughtily refuse. But in a tight market, the seller may feel pressured to accept. If the seller does, you may have made yourself as much as several thousand dollars!

Should I Write in Personal Property That Goes with the Sale? (#9)

When you purchase a home, you are basically buying "real property." Loosely defined, real property is the land, the house, and anything that's permanently attached to it. For example, the windows in the house are real property.

Personal property, on the other hand, is everything else. Furniture is personal property, as are dishes, clothes, and most things that you can take with you.

For most things the definition of what's personal and what's real property is easily grasped and readily agreed to. However, in some circumstances the line between personal and real becomes very fine and that's when you can run into trouble.

For example, wall-to-wall carpeting that is tacked down is normally considered real property—it's permanently attached to the house. But what about a rug that is thrown over the floor and not attached? Normally, it would be considered personal property.

Drapes which are hung on rods are usually considered personal property, if you can take them off without in any way damaging the house. But the rods that hold the drapes and that are affixed by screws into the walls of the house are usually considered real property.

Can you see where problems could arise? You see a house and you fall in love with it. It is completely carpeted and draped. You buy it. But on your final walk-through, all the carpeting is gone, as are the drapes. What happened?

Why, the seller remarks innocently, those were my personal property and I took them along with the furniture.

Is the seller allowed to do that? Probably, if the items weren't permanently attached and if no mention of them was made in the sales agreement.

TIP

If you're ever in the situation just described, you can always say you were led to believe by the seller and the agent that the rugs and drapes were going with the deal and you're not going to complete the purchase until you get them. You may not get them all, but a compromise will probably be reached in which you get some of them. It's not a good solution, but probably the best available to you if you didn't list the personal property in the sales agreement.

Don't assume anything when it comes to items such as rugs, drapes, and even appliances. (Yes, appliances! Most so-called built-in stoves and ovens just pull out and unplug. Unless they are included in a sales agreement, a seller may feel they are personal property too!) Assume they are personal property unless you are specifically told they are not.

It is because of the confusion between personal and real property that today most sales agreements include a clause which states something such as, "all appliances, wall coverings, and floor coverings are included with the purchase except________" and a space is left to write in any exceptions. A separate clause may include all appliances and light fixtures. Look for these clauses in the sales agreement and if they are not there, ask your agent and/or attorney why they are not.

TIP

What should be fairly obvious is that the distinction between personal and real property has many gray areas. Sometimes you can take advantage of these in-between spots. For example, you look at a house and you are impressed with the kitchen. It has been redone and is truly beautiful. There are impressive oak cabinets and a special wall cabinet into which a large two-door refrigerator fits perfectly. You ask about the refrigerator and are told that it, of course, is the personal property of the seller. It's not included in the sale.

But, you think to yourself, where in the world am I ever going to find another refrigerator to fit so perfectly in there? Isn't it a shame that it doesn't go with the house.

Well, of course, you can make it go with the house. When you write up your offer to purchase, indicate that one of the conditions of sale is that the refrigerator goes with the house. No refrigerator, no deal.

What you have done here is convert a piece of personal property into real property through the use of the sales agreement.

Will the sellers accept?

It depends on how anxious they are to sell. If you're the first serious buyer to come along in months, they'll probably grab it. On the other hand, if they've been getting offers every few days, they'll probably turn it down.

Remember, what you're actually doing is offering the sellers a reduction in price equivalent to the cost of the refrigerator. At least that's the way the sellers will see it. (You may want to let the refrigerator go and simply get a lower price.)

The sales agreement (purchase agreement, offer to purchase, deposit receipt) is where you make your deal and define how the purchase process will be followed until the house is yours. Take time with the sales agreement and make sure that you understand it thoroughly.

TIP

The sales agreement is the place where you get a good deal, a mediocre deal, or a deal you'll be kicking yourself about for years after. Don't rush into the sales agreement. Take your time. Check with your attorney. Be sure you're getting all that you can. Be sure you're making the best deal possible.

See more on what goes into a sales agreement in the next chapter.

9
How to Make a Low Offer the Seller Will Accept

Chances are that if you're over 16 years old, you've had the experience of making an offer on an automobile. Perhaps the car was at a dealer's lot. You told the salesperson that you'd like to buy it and, after much coaxing, you agreed to name a price. The salesperson said something like, "Fine, let's write it up."

If your experience(s) are like mine, a very short time later you were in a cubicle in the dealer's inner offices. You might have been pressured by the salesperson to offer perhaps a bit more to get the car. Then you signed the offer, perhaps gave the salesperson a check for a hundred dollars, and waited.

Maybe 15 minutes later a new salesperson entered the office with your offer, shaking her head and saying what a shame it was because the car was so nice, yet the dealer had paid more for it than you were offering. You couldn't really expect the dealer to lose money on the sale, could you? Couldn't you come up with a bit more?

So, by now quite interested in the car, you offered a bit more and then waited again.

This time another individual came to see you. He said he was the sales manager. Yes, your new offer was better, but the dealership had "detailed" (cleaned) the car and had put on new tires, replaced the brakes, and done other work. That had to be paid for.

You argue back and forth. The dealer agrees to take off the new tires and put on some older, but still perfectly safe tires, and you come up with a few more bucks. The sales manager leaves and then you wait some more.

Finally, if you're really getting the full treatment, the "owner" (or someone who says she's the owner) calls on a phone. She sounds angry. She sounds as though she's insulted because you're offering so little. She gives you a price below which she won't sell the car. It's substantially higher than the price you offered. She says it's the best she can do and hangs up.

A few minutes later, the sales manager walks in with a bright smile and congratulates you on your fine negotiating. Now just sign on the dotted line for the price the owner demanded and you'll get your car.

But you're stubborn. You're not going to pay that much. After some not entirely friendly arguing, you get up and leave. You'll find another car elsewhere.

Just as your feet touch the pavement outside the dealership, the original salesperson comes running up. "What happened?" he says. "I thought you were going to buy the car?"

You start telling this friendly and interested person a tale of woes and he says maybe he can do something; after all, his commission is on the line. Just come back into the office and wait a minute.

You go back and wait a few minutes, and then the whole group, except for the owner, appears in the office. They all seem in earnest. What's the highest price you'll go, they want to know?

Feeling intimidated, you name a price between your last offer and the owner's ultimatum. They shake their heads, say that it can't be done. Won't you come up with a few dollars more?

What the heck, you've already invested 5 hours in this. You offer a hundred dollars more. They all disappear. A few minutes later the original salesperson appears. Okay, your offer's accepted. Let's get down to the paperwork.

Query: Did you get a good deal? Or did you get snookered?

Answer? Chances are you got snookered. In some car dealerships, the whole thing is an act, carefully choreographed and planned out ahead of time. You never know what the lowest price the dealer would have sold the car for might be, unless the dealer refuses to sell at your best offer and lets you walk away.

Unless this happens, you'll never know if your offer was really low.

This, of course, is why many Americans hate buying cars. It's the feeling that you're being manipulated. Of course, in many cases, you are. (In response, many one-price dealerships are springing up around the country offering a single sticker price and no negotiating. Saturn dealerships are one example.)

Buying real estate has its similarities. In real estate there usually isn't a troop of agents trying to get you to sign, although in difficult negotiations you may meet and have to deal with not only the agent who showed you the property but the listing agent and the broker of each company involved.

In addition, there are going to be demands on you to come up with a better price, unless you're already offering full (or close to full) price. Just as in buying a car, pressure will be applied to try to get you to move as close to the sales price as possible in order to make a deal.

However, there are significant differences between buying a house and purchasing a car. With a car, the pressures tend to be pretty obvious. With a house, they tend to be more subtle. The real estate agent(s) realizes this may be the biggest investment of your life and handles you very carefully so as not to let your fear of the size of the deal outweigh your desire for the property. Nevertheless, the pressure is there. How well you recognize it and respond to it will determine how good a deal you get. Pressure occurs in three areas:

1. Final price
2. Deposit size
3. Terms

We'll cover each separately. Let's say you've found the house of your dreams. You're now ready to make an offer. How much should you offer?

How Much Should You Offer?

If you ask your agent you may not get the lowest price the seller would accept. Remember, as noted in an earlier chapter, the agent is usually working for the seller (unless you're using a dual or buyer's agent). In addition, the agent doesn't get a commission unless the sale is made and the more you offer, the greater the likelihood that the seller will accept. Consequently, in many ways when you ask your real estate agent how much to offer, you're in a position similar to asking an automobile salesperson how much to offer. You're asking the wrong person.

Whom should you ask?

You can rely on a variety of people to find out what might be the best price to offer on the home of your dreams. Here are some of them.

1. Rely on Yourself

If you've been looking at homes for a while, you should have a pretty good idea what similar houses are listed for. This gives you a good idea of the price range your prospective house is in.

TIP

Selling prices and listing prices are different. Houses rarely sell for what they are listed.

Ask your agent to let you see the selling prices of similar homes going back at least a year. (Any agent worth her salt has these figures readily available from a listing service.) Pick out all sales for similar houses, then try to get as close a match as possible (same number of bedrooms, bathrooms, pool, amenities). In an active market you'll find half a dozen sales or more.

Now, look at the lowest sales price. If it's more than 5 percent lower than the next lowest price, ask the agent why it was so low? Was the house falling down? Did it need a new roof or driveway? Was there some reason for the extremely low price?

If there was and that same reason does not apply to your house, discard that lowest price. If not, my suggestion is that you then offer the lowest price (or less) that any similar house has sold for in the past year.

TRAP

Don't let your agent discourage you from offering a low price. Remember, your agent gets a commission when the deal closes at any price. You get a good deal only when you get your price.

Your agent may argue that the seller certainly won't accept your low price offer. Maybe the seller owes more than you're offering. Maybe the seller has added features which make the house more valuable.

Consider these arguments.

A short sale. It's unlikely a seller will take less than is owed on the house. Yet, in recent recession markets, many sellers did just that—either making up the money on the loans themselves or getting the lenders to write off a portion (called a "short sale") of the mortgage.

Added features. Added features such as a new kitchen or bathroom or other remodeling do add somewhat to the value of the house. (Remember, don't buy a white elephant by purchasing an overbuilt house. Also, don't reimburse the seller for his or her entire costs of remodeling. Except, perhaps, for a very nicely done kitchen or a room addition, it usually just isn't worth it.)

If these arguments make sense, you may want to increase your offer more. On the other hand, if they don't hold water (the listing reveals that the owner does not owe more than your offer; the additions really aren't worth it), stick to your guns.

TIP

Some agents simply refuse a "lowball" offer. They may say something like, "I can't take this offer to the seller. You'll just have to offer more." Baloney. The seller's agent has to take every legitimate offer to the seller. A legitimate offer is one that is in writing with a deposit. Your agent may not like it, but he or she will do it. On the other hand, if the agent is reticent to submit the offer, you'd do better by finding a different agent who is more willing to try to get your price for you.

2. Ask a Different Agent

Another way to determine an appropriate price is to consult with an agent who is in no way involved in the transaction. By the time you get ready to make an offer, you will undoubtedly have worked with several agents. Go back to one who didn't show you the house that you're now considering and have a friendly chat. Make it perfectly clear at the outset that you're going to make an offer through another agent. All you now want is advice.

Remember, agents make a commission only when they are involved in the sale. Thus, this outside agent (who didn't show you the house and who won't write up the offer) has no way to make a commission on the sale—unless the agent can talk you out of making an offer or into making that offer through him.

Thus, you're suddenly going to hear a whole different story. You're going to hear why the property isn't as good as you first thought. You're going to hear how maybe you ought to offer less, a lot less. You'll hear how this agent can get you a better deal than you might otherwise get (through the other agent). You're going to hear things that an agent confident of a sale might not care to say.

Listen, but take it all with a grain of salt. Remember, the agent's motivation remains to get a commission. If you listen between the lines, you might hear what a good offer really should be.

TIP

If you are using a buyer's agent (as described in the last chapter), it is incumbent on that agent to get for you the best price the seller is likely to accept. You can rely much more heavily on a buyer's agent's advice than on a seller's agent's or a dual agent's comments.

3. Ask the Seller

This may come as a surprise to many buyers. "You mean I can talk to the seller?"

Of course you can. The worst the seller can say is, "I'm not discussing the sale. Talk to my agent."

The best the seller can do is to tell you how desperate he or she is and how urgently a sale is needed—and how low an offer might be accepted.

TIP

Your agent isn't likely to encourage you to talk to the seller. That bypasses the agent and arouses all kinds of suspicions (like maybe you're trying to finagle a deal to avoid paying a commission). Don't worry. They won't put you behind bars for talking to the seller. Just remember, the seller is only a phone call away.

TRAP

Don't try to bypass the agent to avoid the commission—even though a seller may suggest this, offering to split the cost of the commission through a lower price. You won't succeed and you'll only offend the agent, who you want to be on your side.

If an agent showed you the property, then almost certainly the house is tied up by an exclusive listing. The only way for the seller to avoid paying a commission is to wait until the listing has expired. Even then, most listing agreements provide that a commission must be paid to an agent for months after the listing expires if the buyer (you) was shown the house during the listing period by the agent.

You would have to wait months in order for this finagling to be effective, and during that time chances are that someone else would come along and buy the property out from under you.

4. Hire an Appraiser

The trouble with hiring an appraiser is that it usually takes too much time and is too expensive (typically $150 to $300). But if you have the time and want a professionally acquired figure for the true market value of the property, you can call in an appraiser.

TIP

Appraisers usually work on a fee basis for lenders. Chances are that if you're going to get a mortgage on the property, you'll need an appraisal anyway. This way, you'll just get it sooner.

TRAP

Not all appraisers are approved by every lender. If you intend to save money on an appraisal by using it for both setting the price and obtaining a mortgage, be sure you know in advance which appraiser your lender uses. Also, cut a deal with the appraiser so you don't get charged twice. Finally, remember that even if you ultimately don't purchase the property, you're still liable for the cost of the appraisal.

Appraisers can be recommended by lenders. They are also listed in the yellow pages of your phone directory. Those who have MAI (American Institute of Real Estate Appraisers) or SREA (Society of Real Estate Appraisers) designations are members of professional appraisal organizations and have usually completed extensive courses in appraising.

TIP

A daring approach is to make an offer with the price contingent upon an appraisal. In other words, you'll agree to accept whatever the appraiser says the property is worth if the seller will likewise accept it. (Usually there are "outs" included which provide that if the price is above a certain point, you won't accept or if it's below a certain point, the seller doesn't have to go through with it.)

A contingent appraisal (described above) is sometimes done with investment properties, but rarely with houses. Nevertheless, if you have a seller who's convinced that the sales price is right and won't budge, it's another alternative. Just be sure that you agree in advance on who the appraiser is and who is to pay the appraisal fee.

How Big a Deposit Should I Give?

Once you've settled on the price, the next consideration for most buyers is the deposit. (This is unfortunate, since the deposit is usually an item of lesser consequence in an offer. Nevertheless, since most buyers worry about it, let's consider it now.)

The deposit is money that you put up at the time you make an offer on a piece of property to show that you are in earnest about buying it. (You're putting your money where your mouth is, so to speak.) Hence the deposit is actually "earnest money." It demonstrates to the seller that your offer isn't capricious. From a seller's perspective, if you say you'll buy a property, it's one thing. If you say you'll buy it and put up $5000 cash, that's something else.

TIP

An offer can be made without a deposit. However, a seller is less likely to accept it. After all, you have very little to lose by not following through on the deal, unless you put up some cash.

Agents, almost universally, insist that you put up a big deposit. They argue that this will convince the seller that you are in earnest about buying the property and that it will help make the deal. While there is a germ of truth here, there is also a lot of chaff.

You can offer any amount as a deposit. Agents often suggest that you offer 1 to 5 percent of the purchase price. On a $100,000 property that's anywhere from $1000 to $5000. If an agent wants you to offer more, it's ridiculous. All that more money will get you is more committed to the deal with less opportunity to back out later on if something sours. Remember, the agent in most cases is working for the seller.

It's to your advantage to offer as little in a deposit as possible, with one exception. That exception is when you have a rather poor offer, but want to demonstrate to the seller that you are sincere. A seller faced with a poor offer may at least consider it if the deposit is big.

TIP

In a hot market, when two essentially similar offers are competing for the same property, a seller is more likely to accept the offer with the big deposit.

TRAP

The money you put up as a deposit is at risk. The less you put up, the less you have at risk.

When I buy property, I rarely put up a deposit of more than 1 percent of the price—unless, of course, it's a poor offer or a hot market. One percent should convince a seller that I'm sincere in most other circumstances.

You Can Add to the Deposit

Sometimes you (or the seller) may want to specify in the sales contract that once the seller has accepted the offer and you've had a chance to inspect and approve the property (and, perhaps once financing has been arranged), you will put up an additional amount of money in the deposit.

Increasing your deposit at a certain specified time in the transaction will sometimes assuage worried sellers about your intentions. It's also of reduced risk to you, since you won't increase the amount until you're assured of the soundness of the deal.

Also, a deposit doesn't have to be in the form of cash. It can be a promissory note or a check that all parties agree not to cash or even personal property such as the title to a car or boat. Cash (cashier's check), however, talks the loudest when you're trying to convince a seller to accept an offer.

TRAP

Sometimes sellers will specify in a listing agreement that they will accept no offers with less than a $5000 deposit, for example. If that's the case, then the agent isn't required to submit offers with less than $5000 as a deposit. Most agents, however, will submit any and all offers.

Will I Get My Deposit Back?

At this point, I'm sure some readers are wondering, "What's the big deal, anyway? Why not put up a bigger deposit? Why not simply go along with what the seller and, perhaps, the agent want? What is the risk?"

Too often buyers simply put their faith in their agent and assume that everything is bound to turn out okay. If the deal sours, they'll get their money back.

In most cases, this is the way it does turn out. But not always. Sometimes when things go bad, they can go bad very quickly, particularly in terms of the deposit.

There are two problem areas you should know about:

1. Who gets the deposit?
2. How do you get it back if the deal falls through?

Who Holds the Deposit?

The seller is entitled to the deposit. However, the seller is the last person in the world you want to give the deposit to. The seller might immediately spend the money, then later on, if the deal falls through, might not be able to refund it to you, even if you're entitled to get it back. It could require the services of an attorney and a lawsuit to secure the return of the deposit and that could be prohibitively expensive. In other words, giving the deposit to the seller is like dropping it down a bottomless pit.

You want the deposit to go to a neutral party who will not frivolously spend the money and who will have it on hand to pay you back, if necessary. The most likely candidate here is the agent.

Giving Your Deposit to an Agent

Real estate agents are required to maintain trust accounts for any money they receive. In other words, they can't commingle your money with their own, but must hold it in a separate account in trust for you. The problem is that, in theory, the deposit belong to the seller and if the seller demands it, the agent is supposed to hand the deposit over. Most agents, however, are as wary of the seller as you are and will do everything possible to hold the money in trust until the offer is accepted and the deal closes.

TIP

In most states the most common reason for real estate license suspension or revocation is the commingling of funds in a trust account. It's not that agents are dishonest; it's that they are sometimes lousy accountants.

However, to ensure that they don't lose their license, almost always they will bend over backward to repay any money stuck in their trust account. Further, many states have special recovery funds. If you lose money through the carelessness (or fraud) of an agent, you may be able to recover it from the state, even though it could take years. Check with your state's department of real estate.

Giving Your Deposit to an Escrow Company

Today, many very good agents realize that accepting a check for a deposit puts them at great risk. If the deal doesn't go through, both the buyer and the seller may demand the money, leaving the agent in the middle. To avoid this, shrewd agents suggest you write the deposit check out to an escrow company which, you agree in advance, will handle the escrow of the property once the seller accepts. In other words, give the deposit to a neutral party. Sound good?

There is a peril here. It is that after the seller accepts, the deal can still fall apart through no fault of your own. If that happens you could have trouble getting your money back, even from a neutral escrow.

The reason is that escrows simply handle the documents and funds in a transaction. In order for an escrow to operate, *all* parties involved must agree to the escrow's instructions. If, for example, you tell the escrow to return your money and the seller tells the escrow to hold onto it or to turn it over to the seller, there's no agreement. And your money remains in limbo.

This affects you far more than the seller. After all, it's your money. Many sellers are content to let the money sit in an inactive escrow for months just to "punish" a buyer for a deal that falls through.

Fortunately, calmer minds often prevail and sellers usually will agree to release your funds, once they become convinced that there's no way they can get the money and that to continue to hold it might result in a lawsuit against them.

TRAP

Making your check payable to an escrow does ensure that it goes to a neutral party. It does not, however, ensure that you'll get it back quickly or easily.

What If the Deal Falls Through?

What must be obvious by now is that putting up a deposit is a sometimes tricky thing which can have significant consequences. How do you get the deposit back, for example, if the deal doesn't go through?

There are two considerations here: First, why didn't the deal go through? If it's your fault, you may not be entitled to a return of the deposit. Second, if you are entitled to a return, how do you get the funds transferred back to you?

TIP

Operating on the principle that the time to consult an attorney is before you need one, I advise you to seek the services of a professional real estate lawyer at this juncture. Chances are you're going to need one anyway before the deal is concluded, and by bringing the lawyer in at an early stage, you could avoid much grief. (Most lawyers who deal in real estate have set fees that are much lower than for general legal work. Ask the lawyer in advance what the fees are.)

If the Seller Doesn't Accept Your Offer

If the seller does not accept your offer, you're entitled to your deposit back. It's just that simple.

The seller has to agree to your entire offer, including any terms you propose. If the seller agrees to the price but not the terms and counters with different terms, which you don't accept, there's no deal and you're entitled to your money back. If the seller accepts your terms but counters with a different price, which you don't accept, the deal's off and you're entitled to your deposit back.

The moment the seller declines your offer and "counters" (proposes a deal different in some way, no matter how small), the deal is dead. Unless you accept the seller's counteroffer, you're entitled to your deposit back. (We'll have more to say about what constitutes acceptance, and what doesn't, shortly.)

TRAP

Once in a very great while an unscrupulous agent will say something such as, "Even though the seller didn't accept, I made a good-faith effort to get the deal through. Therefore, I'm entitled to half the deposit. I'll return half to you and keep the other half." No way. The agent gets a commission only if the deal is consummated. If the seller never agrees, no commission is due. Politely tell the agent you want your entire deposit back immediately or you will report the agent to the state department of real estate. That should do it.

If the Seller Accepts and Then, Later on, the Deal Falls Through Because of You

There are many reasons the deal might fall through because of your fault. For example, you could be counting on Aunt Harriet to give you the money for the down payment. You get the seller to sign an offer, secure financing, and poor Aunt Harriet has a heart attack and dies. Her money will be tied up in probate for years. Sure, you didn't do anything intentionally to quash the deal, but you don't have the expected money to perform. As far as the seller is concerned, it's your fault.

Or you get cold feet. You take a look at those huge monthly payments and you decide that you can't go through with it. You want out, period.

Or you find another house that is really perfect. You want to get out of this deal so that you can get the other.

Or...

There are lots of reasons, good and bad, that you might not want or be able to perform on your end of a purchase agreement. The point here is, however, that for whatever reason, it's your fault the deal doesn't go forward. What are your chances of getting the deposit back?

Put simply, your chances are not good.

In fact, you could be in hot water and liable for a lot more than just the deposit, as we'll see shortly.

Most sales agreements provide that if you default, the seller is entitled to keep the deposit. Separately, agreements between seller and agent specify that they will split the deposit in the event of your default. Thus, at least in theory, as soon as you default on the deal, your deposit is lost. Unfortunately, it may not end there.

In addition, the seller may sue you. After the seller accepts your offer and you default (refuse to buy), the seller can sue you for specific performance. That means the seller can sue to force you to buy. Since, for practical purposes, this is most unlikely (it's hard to force someone to buy something), the seller could sue for money equivalent to the price of the property—as well as damages—and possibly win.

In the past when a buyer defaulted, a seller occasionally did sue for damages, thus tying up the courts and causing long-term problems for everyone concerned. As a result, liquidated-damage clauses for residential real estate (buyer occupied) have come into use in sales agreements and are accepted and even codified in many states.

Liquidated Damages

Basically these clauses state that if you and the seller agree in advance, the deposit (or a portion of it) will constitute the entire damages the seller is entitled to in the event of your default. In other words, you agree in advance that the seller can keep the deposit, provided she or he agrees not to sue you for additional damages or specific performance.

Many states put limitations on liquidated damages. In order to keep more, the seller has to prove in a court of law that it's reasonable to hang onto the money. If you want your money back, you have to prove that it's reasonable for you to get it. Either way, for practical purposes, the seller is usually satisfied and unless you're litigious by nature, you probably are too. (Of course, both seller and buyer can agree to virtually any amount as liquidated damages, though it's normally not to your advantage as buyer to agree to a higher amount.)

TRAP

You may be asked to sign or initial a clause in the sales agreement that states that if you do not go through with the sale, your deposit is automatically forfeited in exchange for the seller not suing you for specific performance. Should you sign? Ask an attorney. A lot depends on the specific deal and your financial situation.

TIP

Don't enter into a contract to buy real estate unless you plan to perform. If you have doubts, leave a way out for yourself via a "contingency clause," to be discussed later.

Extenuating Circumstances

While what potentially can or cannot happen may seem quite dire, what actually happens in practice can be somewhat different. If you simply back out because you change your mind or find a better house, chances are that neither the agent nor the seller is going to be sympathetic and you stand an excellent chance of losing your deposit.

However, if circumstances cause you to default—your aunt, whom you were counting on for money, dies or you get sick or injured or something happens which is truly beyond your control—then it's often a different story. Here, you are truly relying on the goodwill of the agent and the seller. In almost every case I have seen of this happening, the buyer has gotten the deposit back.

Agents are not in the business to make money on deposits. Sellers are interested in selling, not in keeping the deposit of a person who falls on hard times. I have seen agents bend over backward in these circumstances to get the seller to give the deposit back. I have seen sellers gladly return the deposit, sometimes over the agent's objections. Of course, you could get the bad apples, but goodwill in people is everywhere. So if you default because of circumstances beyond your control, chances are you'll get most, if not all, of your deposit back.

If the Seller (Not You) Fails to Go Through with the Deal

Why would a seller fail to go through with a deal, once signed? Simple. You offer $150,000 for a house and the seller accepts. Two days later another buyer comes in with an offer of $175,000.

Wouldn't it be wonderful if the seller could get out of your deal and accept the new one? The seller would stand to make an additional $25,000. That's plenty of reason to default.

In these circumstances you are fully entitled to the return of your deposit. In addition, you may want to sue the seller for specific performance, to force a sale to you. (After all, you could then resell for the higher price and keep the profit yourself!)

When the seller defaults, there's not much concern about getting the deposit back. Usually the seller is more than happy to do everything to get that deposit back to you in the hope that you won't take further action.

TIP

You can refuse to accept the deposit back. Tell the agent that you insist on buying the property and that you'll hold the seller to the exact terms of the deal. This should tie up the property at the least.

If you're really not all that interested in the property, the worst you might do is get a cash settlement from the seller. Remember, however, that as a practical matter it's difficult to force the sale of a house when the seller is determined not to sell, even when you're in the right. It's also "iffy" to press a lawsuit, since the seller might be able to find "outs" in the purchase agreement. Again, check with your attorney.

Rather than drag the whole thing into litigation, which could take years to resolve and in which there is no guarantee you'll prevail, I usually just take the deposit back (and any settlement the agent and seller may offer) and look elsewhere.

If It's No One's Fault, but the Deal Just Can't Be Made

There are a lot of reasons that a deal might not go through. You may not be able to secure adequate financing. The title to the property may not be clear. There could be extensive termite damage. It could turn out that the house is in the middle of a flood plain.

The reasons are endless and they crop up in a good many deals. In most cases there's a way to work them out. Other financing is secured. The seller clears the title. The termite damage is fixed. You agree to accept the risk of flood damage for a lower price, and so on. In other words, the problems are solved one way or another.

However, sometimes it just doesn't work and there's no deal to be made. What happens to your deposit then?

If you've given it to an agent who has kept it in a personal trust account, you can demand it back and in most cases the agent will immediately return it (perhaps risking the ire of the seller). If the conditions of the purchase agreement can't be met, you're entitled to get it back and most agents don't want to argue the point.

On the other hand, if the deposit's been placed in an escrow account, it takes both buyer's and seller's agreement to get it out. Maybe the seller is angry that the deal fell through and says, "I'm not signing anything."

There your deposit sits, even though you're perfectly entitled to it. Unless the agent can prevail and convince the seller to release it, it could remain there for years!

As a practical matter, however, as soon as another buyer comes along, the seller probably will be forced to release it so as not to jeopardize a later sale.

TIP

Here is one possible method of avoiding the tying up of the deposit in escrow if the sale does not go through: Make sure the escrow instructions provide that should the deal not be consummated within a specified period of time (90 days, for example) because any of the conditions of sale cannot be met, the escrow will automatically return the deposit to you. Thus, if the deal doesn't go through, you automatically get your money back. The trouble is, most sellers see this arrangement as a way for you, the buyer, to weasel out of the deal and will refuse to go along with it. It's a great method to use, if you can. However, your choice may often be between insisting on such a clause and losing the deal or just allowing your money to go into escrow and taking your chances.

All of which brings us back to my original point. The money you put up for deposit is at risk. The less you put up, the less you risk.

TIP

If you're worried about getting your deposit back, put up a smaller deposit. If the seller insists on a large deposit, offer to increase the deposit at a later time.

What Terms Should I Offer?

The terms of a purchase are often more important than the price. Thus, this is an area of vital concern to you, the buyer.

TIP

Sellers are often hung up on price. Offer them their full price and they may give you ridiculously favorable terms.

Your agent is likely to insist that you offer terms which basically protect you. For example, the agent may want to include a clause that allows you to receive your deposit money back, and to get out of the deal, if you cannot secure financing. Usually this is a wise idea.

On the other hand, the agent is not likely to want to include terms which are far more to your benefit and which would allow you to back out of the deal anytime you wanted. The agent's goal (particularly if you're dealing with a seller's agent), after all, is to tie you into the deal as strongly as possible. Remember, the agent normally gets a commission only if the deal is consummated.

Financing Terms

Most of the terms of a purchase agreement are going to revolve around the financing. Will you get the mortgage money from an outside lender? Will you want the seller to finance all or part of your purchase? What interest rate and term will you insist upon for the mortgage?

TIP

It's not enough to simply provide that you must secure a mortgage or there is no deal. It's important that the terms of the mortgage be spelled out. For example:

1. The mortgage will be for $100,000 (or whatever amount).
2. The interest rate will not exceed 8 percent (or whatever rate is current).
3. The term of the mortgage will be for 30 years (or 15 or whatever).
4. It will be a "fixed" mortgage (or "adjustable" or some other type).
5. Other specifics.

Indicating exactly what type of mortgage you are to get protects you and gives you a way out should financing not be available.

Financing is treated separately in Chapter 11, but for now it's important to point out that the more "contingencies" you add regarding the mortgage, the less likely the seller is to go along with the deal. Consider, there are two buyers for the same house. The first offers all cash (meaning that the buyer is going to find her own financing and guarantees to conclude the deal without regard to finance). The second is your offer, which is for 20 percent down with the sale contingent on your securing financing.

Which is the stronger offer? If you were the seller, which would you take?

If I were the seller, I'd surely take the first offer. There the buyer is saying that she is not worried about financing and it's not contingent on the sale. In the second the buyer is saying she doesn't know about financing. Maybe it can be secured—and then, maybe not. The first offer is a sure deal (or at least an almost sure forfeit of deposit if the deal doesn't go through). The second deal is a maybe, until you're able to secure financing.

TIP

As noted earlier, in a hot market, a wise buyer will obtain preliminary approval for financing from a lender before looking for a house. Then when the house is found, in order to knock out competitive bidders, the buyer will show the letter of preapproval. In a desperate case, the buyer may simply come in with an "all cash" offer. This, however, remains extremely risky because you never know for sure that you'll get financing until the money is funded. However, it impresses sellers immensely.

Making a Full-Price Offer

Another way to knock out competition or to get better terms is to offer the seller full price. As noted earlier, sellers are almost always hung up on price. If they think they're getting their price, then they're happy, no matter how unfavorable the terms may be.

After offering full price, insist that the seller carry back a second mortgage (or first) at a lower-than-market interest rate for longer than a normal term. For example, write in a second mortgage for 5 percent when the going rate is 8 percent, and make it for 10 years when the normal term is 5. Why would a seller agree to such favorable (to you) financing? Because you're offering full price!

TIP

The few thousand dollars you don't get knocked off the price may be more than offset by far lower payments over the term of the mortgage.

Time Terms

There are other terms of serious importance to you. One of the most crucial is time. How long do you have to secure financing, to come up with the down payment and closing costs, to close the escrow?

Time is often negotiated. Perhaps the seller wants 90 days before moving out. That suits you fine, so there is immediate agreement.

On the other hand, perhaps the seller wants to close escrow in 30 days, but you feel you'll need 90 to raise the cash for the down payment. Now time is a negotiating point. You compromise. You'll take a chance on coming up with the cash in 60 days, but the seller has to be willing to lower the price $1000 or throw in the refrigerator.

The seller balks and says the most he can go is 45 days, but he'll lower the interest rate on the second mortgage he's carrying from

9 percent to 8 percent and throw in the refrigerator. Is it okay with you?

Now you have to make a judgment call. The agent may suggest a "bridge" loan (temporary financing until you can get your cash) to cover the extra time you'll need. But this costs you extra money.

In the final analysis, you'll have to weigh all the factors regarding time. Just remember it's a negotiating card, one which only you can play.

Other Terms

There are a host of other terms in a real estate transaction, almost all of which are negotiable. For example, you may agree to pay full price for a property *if* the seller agrees to pay your closing costs.

Or you'll buy only if the seller agrees to pay for the termite inspection as well as any repair work.

Or…?

Throughout all this you can generally rely on the real estate agent to see that you don't get into anything that would really hurt you. (After all, unfavorable terms might result in problems for the agent down the road.) On the other hand, you can't expect the agent to fight too hard to help you get very favorable terms (particularly if it's a seller's agent). After all, the more the terms favor you, the harder it is for the agent to get the seller to agree. I've never met an agent who wanted to work hard closing a deal.

Thus, it's up to you to get the best terms.

As noted earlier, the time to consult an attorney is before you need one. At this juncture a real estate attorney can prove extremely useful. The attorney can create a purchase agreement that protects you and gives you most favorable terms.

TRAP

Beware of attorneys who work too hard for your interests. In general, real estate agents dread attorneys, not because they don't protect people, but because they tend to muck up deals. There's an old saying among real estate agents that the fastest way to have a deal go sour is to bring in an attorney.

Yes, you want your rights protected and you want the most favorable terms. But you also want to be able ultimately to purchase the house. An attorney can create a sales contract so favorable to you that no seller will accept it.

As with the ancient Greeks, moderation is in order. Allow your attorney to draw up the terms correctly. But use your own common sense when it comes to which terms to include.

Should I Insert Contingency Clauses?

A contingency clause is essentially any clause in a contract that says the offer depends or hinges on some other event or action. For example, wording that would say, "This offer is contingent upon the buyer winning the state lottery" is a legitimate contingency clause, one that obviously no sane seller would accept.

I once knew a builder whose advice was, "No matter what the contract, always be sure that somewhere in it, it says, 'subject to.' I don't care what comes after the 'subject to,' just as long as it's in there."

The words "subject to" have a meaning similar to "contingent." They make the sales offer hinge on some event or action. What my builder friend meant was that as long as those words were in it, he could get out of the contract if he had to. He had many experiences fighting subcontractors, landowners, and others and I firmly believe to this day that he could get out of any contract with those words in it. For your purposes, however, a contingency clause is very useful to protect you against an unforeseen change of condition.

Some contingencies are absolutely necessary for the sales agreement and few agents would hesitate to put them in. For example, you might have a contingency clause that read: "This offer contingent on the Buyers completing the sale of their current home at 123 Maple St., Ft. Wayne, Indiana, for $100,000 within 60 days of seller's acceptance of this offer." (*Note:* Do not rely on this language—consult your attorney.)

The idea here is that if you, the buyer, don't sell your current house, you aren't committed to purchasing the new one. To make sure this is fully understood, the following language is sometimes added, "If this condition of sale is not satisfied within the specified time, Buyer may cancel agreement and receive deposit back. Cancellation is to be by written notice. If no such notice is given, this condition shall be considered waived."

The obvious purpose here is to protect you as much as possible. Keep in mind, however, that many sellers will not accept such contingencies. After all, why should they tie up their house while you're trying to sell yours? Of course, if the market's slow, they may be willing. But in a hot market, forget it.

Selling One House to Buy Another

I once worked with another agent in the sale of my own house and the purchase of another. I wrote in a contingency clause similar to the one noted above. The agent objected. She said, "You'll never get the sellers to sign. Besides, the market's strong. You'll sell your house. Why worry? Just agree to buy the other one without the clause."

Fortunately, I refused. The sellers didn't and the deal was made.

As it turned out, I did sell my house later, but found it would take an additional 60 days for the sale to be completed (a total of about 80 days). The contingency clause was for only 60 days. Near the end of the 60 days I sent a letter to the sellers saying I had not completed the sale of my house and I was cancelling the agreement. However, I did have a buyer for my property and if the sellers would give me an additional 45 days, I could conclude the sale.

The sellers fumed and ranted, but what could they do? I had every right to cancel the deal. On the other hand, if they agreed to an extension, they would still sell their house. Of course they agreed.

On the other hand, consider what would've happened without that contingency clause. I'd have been forced to try to make the purchase of the new house without the sale of my existing property or face losing my deposit and potentially having to pay damages. The sellers would be under no pressure to give me an extension of time.

The agent advised me badly. She wanted only a quick sale. Since the contingency weakened the sale, she advised against it. Whose interest was she looking out for in this case?

House Inspection

Unless it's otherwise already covered in the sales agreement, you should insist upon your approval of a professional house inspection as a contingency. House inspectors are listed in the yellow pages of your phone book. (See Chapter 13 for more details.) They can go through and tell you if there are any problem areas in the house such as plumbing, electrical, heating, air conditioning, and so forth.

The cost is usually only a few hundred dollars, and in most cases in today's market the sellers will be willing to pay for it! (The sellers are willing because an inspection protects them against hidden problems when they warrant the house to be in good condition.)

TRAP

Be sure that your purchase is contingent on your *approving* the inspection report. Otherwise, you may find out that there's trouble and still be committed to purchase without it getting fixed!

Preclosing Inspection

Most buyers today want the right to inspect the property (walk through) just before the deal closes. You want to be sure that it's still exactly the same way it was when you first saw it and that the sellers haven't damaged it or removed something.

Sellers don't like this contingency, because it can leave you a way out. Therefore, they usually want to insist that while you can see the property, you don't have the right to back out if it's the same as it was originally.

The trouble is, what one person considers the same, another may consider different. If you don't have the right to back out, your final inspection is worthless.

TIP

Make sure that your preclosing inspection is "contingent." If you don't approve the property, either the sellers correct the problem or there's no deal.

Frivolous Contingency Clauses

As buyers have become more aware of contingency clauses, they have tried with increasing frequency to have them inserted into purchase agreements.

TIP

Whenever possible, leave yourself a way out of a purchase agreement. You never know what's going to happen and you might need it.

The trouble is that at the same time sellers have become increasingly wary of such clauses in agreements. Sellers want to know that their property is sold. They don't want to take it off the market on a presumed sale only to learn 2 months later that the buyer is backing out, without penalty, because of a contingency clause.

Thus in today's market only realistic contingency clauses are likely to be accepted, not frivolous ones. What are frivolous contingency clauses which sellers are unlikely to accept? Here are a few:

> "This purchase is contingent on the Buyer's grandmother inspecting and approving the property." (Two months later grandma looks at the property and disapproves—no deal.)
>
> "This purchase is contingent upon the buyer securing a first mortgage at 3 percent per annum." (The current rate is 7 percent—no deal here.)
>
> "This purchase is contingent on the buyer's approval of a soil and structural inspection of the property." (The buyer can simply disapprove even a good inspection.)

I hope you get the idea. Whenever the sale is contingent upon some outside event that the buyer controls, it's really a wide open deal from which the buyer can back out at virtually any time. In the real world sellers rarely accept such contingencies.

However, smart sellers will accept frivolous contingencies by limiting them. The most common form of limitation, as noted above, is time. Yes, you can have your grandmother look at the property or have an inspection. But it must be done within 7 days of the seller's acceptance. If you haven't given the seller written notice of disapproval within 7 days, it is assumed you have approved and the contingency is removed.

What this does is give you, the buyer, some time, but not limitless time. In this case once the 7 (or however many) days have passed, either you bite the bullet and purchase the property or walk away from it.

How Do I Get Help on Contingency Clauses?

Your real estate agent should be able to help on contingency clauses. Just remember, however, that your agent is trying to close the deal, to be sure there is a sale. Hence the agent's interests may not be in giving you as many "outs" as possible. They may be quite the opposite. An attorney you hire, on the other hand, will be most interested in seeing that you have as many options as possible.

10 Counteroffers: The Art of Bargaining

I once had a friend who was a master at making offers on houses. She would make the offer favorable to her in all areas—price, terms, time, contingencies, personal property—every area you could name. There was nothing left to favor the seller.

Of course, the sellers almost always turned down her offers. But they also almost always counteroffered. They came back with a compromise which was sometimes much less than they had been asking. Many times that counter was just what my friend actually wanted out of the deal. She had mastered the art of bargaining.

TIP

Often you may be able to get what you want in price or terms not by demanding it up front, but by going for a counteroffer. The counteroffer can be your most important tool when bargaining.

How Do Counteroffers Work?

Counteroffers occur when the seller turns down your original offer, but then sends you back a sales agreement that offers different price, terms, or virtually anything else that departs from your original offer.

Counteroffer Procedure

The procedure is quite simple. Assuming you're using an agent:

1. You make an offer which the agent and/or attorney writes up.
2. The agent presents the offer as soon as possible to the sellers.
3. The sellers either accept the offer exactly as presented or turn it down.
4. If the sellers turn down the offer, they may make a counteroffer to you.
5. You may now accept their counteroffer or turn it down. If you turn it down, you may counter back.
6. This countering can go on almost indefinitely. Sometimes it gets down to arguing over a washing machine or repainting one wall of a living room.
7. The deal is made only when both you and the seller accept the same counteroffer.

TIP

Whenever a seller counters with any kind of change at all, it is a new offer. You now have the option of walking away from the deal with your deposit and no strings attached.

What Are the Strategies for Counteroffering?

There are at least three different kinds of strategies when it comes to counteroffers. We'll consider all three here.

The Terrible Offer

In the opening example of this chapter we talked about a buyer who purposely made very unfavorable offers to sellers in the hopes they would counter with a compromise offer that was still far below what they were asking. This is a strategy, also called "lowballing" the seller, which sometimes works. However, it is also fraught with peril. Remember, the seller may be insulted by the low offer and simply turn it down out of hand and not counter.

TIP

Lowball offers are seldom accepted. But occasionally a desperate seller, afraid of losing the first real buyer to come along in months, will accept one. Don't overlook the terrible lowball offer. Sometimes it can net you a terrific deal.

If a seller turns down your terrible offer and refuses to counter, what do you do?

My friend, noted above, would simply forget the property and move on. Her philosophy was that there were many more houses for sale than buyers and a better deal was always waiting just around the corner.

If you can feel comfortable about walking away from the house you're offering on, then perhaps the "terrible offer" is the way for you to go. The trouble, however, is that most of us fall in love with a house. Once we decide to make an offer, we've committed ourselves to getting that house no matter what.

Thus, when we make a "terrible offer" and the sellers turn us down cold, we're in a bad position. Instead of walking away, we want to stay and play—we want that house.

Now, to get the property, we must eat humble pie and make a better offer. If we really want the place, that's our only alternative.

This, however, lets the sellers know something that we desperately want to keep very secret. It lets them know that we are eager to buy their house. Why else would we come back with a stronger offer after they've turned us down cold? Now the sellers are likely to hold out for their terms, price, and just about everything else. They are far less inclined to compromise. The "terrible offer" strategy has painted us into a corner from which there is little escape.

The Wonderful Offer

Okay, the point is well taken. You really want the house. Therefore, you should make the very best offer you can, right? Figure out what is the highest price you can pay, the best terms you can offer, and so on. In other words, you offer the sellers the most favorable offer (to them) that you can.

Great, except that unless you're offering full price and the exact terms the sellers want (or darn close), you probably still won't get the house. Why? It's simple.

No matter what you offer, if it's less than exactly what the sellers are asking, you'll probably get a counteroffer. Many sellers automatically assume that your first offer is just that—a first trial position. They assume that if they come down a little bit, you'll come up.

The sellers will likely counter with a price higher than you offered plus better terms (for them), and then where do you go? You've already given everything you can give. There's nothing left. You can't offer more money or better terms. The best you can do is send the agent back with your original offer saying, "Take it or leave it—the buyers can't do better."

Depending on the market, the sellers may leave it.

The Compromise Offer

Somewhere in between the "terrible offer" and the "wonderful offer" is the compromise offer. This is an offer which you don't expect the sellers to accept, but which you hope will set the stage for a bargaining process that will get you the property at a price and terms you can afford and are willing to pay.

TIP

Don't expect the agent to lead you to the compromise offer. Most agents in my experience suggest the buyer make the "wonderful offer." The agent is thinking in the back of her mind that this is most likely to get the seller to sign, or at least counter. And when the seller counters, you the buyer will always be willing to come up with more. In other words, the agent may be manipulating you to spend more than you can or want.

How do you know what to put into the "compromise offer"? What price, terms, and so forth should it be? We discussed this at some length in terms of actual figures in an earlier chapter. Now, however, in terms of strategy, here's what I suggest.

Try to make the lowest offer to which the seller will make a *serious* counter. The easiest area to demonstrate countering is in terms of price. The market is firm and we'll say the sellers are asking $120,000 for the property. Similar houses are selling in the $115,000 to $125,000 range. They're asking a fair price.

If you offer $95,000 the sellers are going to think you're trying to steal it and either may not counteroffer or may simply counter at, perhaps, $119,500, very close to full price. In other words, they may not close you out (by not countering), but they aren't willing to compromise much either.

On the other hand, if you offer $110,000, for example, you're very close to the bottom range for houses in the area. The sellers may realize that what you're doing is trying to determine if they are willing to accept the lower end of the price range, or about $115,000.

To most sellers this will seem a serious offer to which they should make a serious counter. Of course, they could simply hold to their price. Or, if they're serious about selling, they might counter at, say, $116,000.

Now you're getting somewhere. You may simply want to accept this counteroffer and end the dickering. However, if you're really inclined to get the most, now you'll up the ante, but only a bit. Perhaps you'll offer $111,000. The sellers have come down $4000, you've gone up $1000.

The sellers very quickly will see where this is going. $5000 separates you. They may suspect that you want them to come down another $4000 while you'll go up only $1000 more, settling on a price of around $112,000.

This will upset most sellers and very likely they will now make their best counteroffer. It might simply be $115,000, the lower end of the price range for their type of house. Or they might split the difference, offering $2500 less, or $113,500. In any event, this is likely to be as low as they go.

What should you do?

When the compromising reaches this stage, my suggestion is to accept the sellers' offer, if you're in love with the house. It may indeed be as low as they will go. If you try to get the "last drop of blood" and counter again, they may simply wash their hands of it and you may end up not getting the property.

TRAP

Don't paint yourself into a corner. If you only make counteroffers that favor you, you could lose. If you're determined to have the house, you're better off making a counter that contains enough bones for the sellers so that if they don't accept, at least they'll counter back.

TIP

The goal in bargaining is to keep the ball in play. You always want there to be a counteroffer somewhere en route. The moment either you or the sellers stop countering, the deal is dead.

Getting the Counteroffer Accepted

There are a few strategies about offers and counteroffers that you should know about. Sometimes, these can save you money, if not a deal.

Timing the Offer

When you make an offer to a seller, it is open-ended. That means that you've written down the price, the terms, and any other conditions that you want and that you agree to be bound by them. If the seller accepts and communicates that acceptance to you, you're on the hook.

However, things change. The house you're in love with today may not be so appealing tomorrow. Yet another home may come along that really turns you on next week. Your financial condition could change. Therefore, you don't want to make this open-ended offer last forever. You want to set a time limit on it. The offer is good, for example, for 3 days only. After that, it's null and void.

The sales agreement normally will include a space for you to fill in the time limit for the offer. Be sure *not* to leave this space blank.

TRAP

Sometimes agents will encourage you put in a long period of time—4 to 5 days or even a week—for acceptance to take place. They may say that it will take that long to convince the sellers to sign.

This approach makes sense only if the sellers are out of town and even then it may only be marginally good advice, especially with fax machines and express mailing services readily available. Remember, the more time the sellers have to think about it, the more time there is for someone to come in with a better offer.

Giving the sellers a lot of time to accept is simply cutting your own throat.

TIP

One of the most successful real estate agents I know would insist that his buyers give the sellers only 1 day and that was the same day that the offer was made. In other words, if you made the offer at 5 o'clock that evening, the sellers had only until 12 o'clock that same night to sign. Otherwise, the offer was no longer valid!

Buyers used to protest, saying, "What if the sellers want to think about it?"

The agent would respond, "The more the sellers think about it, the more likely they are to find reasons to not sign."

Buyers would ask, "But doesn't that put the sellers on the spot?"

To which the agent would reply, "Certainly. That's the whole point. The short time forces the sellers to make a decision here and now."

Finally buyers would worry, "Won't the sellers think the offer is frivolous, being made with so short a time for acceptance?"

"Quite the contrary," the agent would reply. "A short time period for acceptance shows you mean business. It implies that if the sellers don't accept the offer right away (presumably as written) you'll go elsewhere."

You know something? That agent was right. He got more buyers' offers accepted without changes or with minor counters than any other agent I ever knew. Think about it.

Can I Withdraw My Offer?

It's important to understand that although your offer is open-ended (you're committed; the sellers aren't—until they sign) and although it has a defined time limit for acceptance, you do not have to keep it open. Anytime before the sellers sign *and that acceptance is conveyed to you,* you can withdraw the offer.

You make an offer at 5 o'clock that the agent will present to the sellers at 8 o'clock. At 8:30, you call the sellers' house and ask the agent if they've accepted. He says he's just presented it and they're thinking about it. They'll probably sign in a few minutes. You instruct him to withdraw the offer immediately. The offer is no longer good.

Why would you want to withdraw an offer? There are lots of reasons. Soon after submitting an offer, you find a better house at a better price. You want out of the offer immediately.

Or, perish the thought, you or a family member has a car accident or you discover that you have a debilitating disease and you don't want to go through with the deal.

Or you're simply being fickle.

It doesn't matter. You don't have to have a reason. You can withdraw the offer anytime before acceptance is communicated to you.

Has Acceptance Been Communicated to You?

Remember, it's not good enough for the sellers to have signed your offer. That acceptance must be communicated to you. In practice, this is done in two ways. Usually the agent will immediately call you to tell you the sellers have accepted your offer and shortly thereafter follow it up by presenting a copy of the offer to you that has been signed by the sellers.

Technically, communication isn't complete until you get that copy signed by the sellers, but in the real world, calling and telling you usually is what is done by most agents.

Keep in mind that the offer is accepted only if it is unchanged. If even one word or one dollar has been changed, the offer has not been accepted.

TRAP

Many first-time buyers are unaware of the important subtleties of unaccepted offers. I have seen agents get sellers to make a counteroffer, then call the buyer and say, "Congratulations—your offer was accepted! Only the seller made a few changes which I'll need to drop by and have you initial. I'll explain it to you when I get there."

That's wrong. If the seller changes anything, it's a new offer—totally and completely. A counteroffer is just that. It's a new offer that the seller is making. *You are under no obligation to accept a counteroffer, no matter how close to your original offer it may be.*

Sellers are at great risk when they make counteroffers because they are, in effect, rejecting your offer and substituting another for it. When this happens, the tables are turned. The sellers may give you a time limit to accept their counteroffer and you can do with it what you will. (Just remember, if you counter the counter, once again the ball's in the other court.)

What Form Should the Counteroffer Take?

In the old days, sales agreements had so little printed on them that it was a simple matter to "X" out the undesirable conditions and then write in new ones. (In other words, there were plenty of open spaces available.) Frequently a counteroffer that had gone back and forth a number of times had so many changes and buyers' and sellers' initials scribbled on it that it was hard to read and difficult to determine what the final conditions were.

That was the trouble. Should there be a dispute later on, the sales agreement, which is the document that makes the deal, wasn't reliable.

As a result, as noted earlier, today's sales agreement has very little room to write in anything. Most of it is printed material and boxes that can be checked or have dollar amounts entered. It is very difficult to write a counter on such a document.

TIP

It is good strategy to make the counteroffer (either your own or the sellers') on the same document as the original offer. The reason is psychological. When the sellers counter on the same document, even though you may know that their counter rejects your original offer, using the same document makes it somehow seem like you're closer than before.

When you counter the sellers' counteroffer, putting it on the same document does the same thing for the seller.

TRAP

Some agents use sales agreements that have a separate section on the last page which reads, "Seller's Counteroffer." The idea here is that this is the designated place for the sellers to write in their counter.

I think this is a bad idea. It encourages sellers to think that a counteroffer is warranted. A sales agreement with no specific place for the counter, on the other hand, implies that it should be accepted.

How Do I Make a Counter-Counteroffer?

There are basically three alternatives for the form of a counter-counteroffer. The first is to write up a new offer on a new document. This is the least desirable alternative for the reasons stated earlier—it tends to throw negotiations back to square one.

The second alternative is to scribble changes on the sales agreement itself. This also is not a good idea because of the way the forms are created today. The changes very quickly become illegible.

The third and what I think is usually best alternative is to turn the form over and write the counteroffer on the back of the original. (Or, if this is impossible, use a separate sheet which can then be attached to and made a part of the sales agreement document.)

Most agents are quite adroit at setting up counters. A typical form for countering is to have the seller sign the front of the sales agreement and then have a clause by the signature which reads something like this:

> All the terms and conditions set out on the face of the contract are acceptable to the seller in their entirety, with the following corrections or changes: 1__________, 2__________....

Remember, this is in effect a rejection of your offer. It is a counteroffer which you may or may not want to accept. But you are not bound to accept it.

If you like it, but want further changes, then have your attorney or agent write in something similar with changes that you demand.

When Should I Stop Countering?

Sometimes you and the sellers are so far off on price or terms that it becomes obvious that there is no real room for compromise. For example, the best offer you can make is $112,000 and the best counter the seller can make is $120,000. Sometimes you have to accept the fact that not all deals can be made.

TIP

Refusing to counter can be a bargaining tool. After several counteroffers you're still apart on price or terms. Instead of accepting the sellers' most recent counter, you do a "walkaway" and send it back. You include a signed statement to the effect that your last counteroffer (the one before the sellers made their most recent counter) is your final and best offer. You'll give the sellers until midnight to accept it or you're no longer interested in the property. Further, you're not interested in any more counteroffers from the sellers.

The idea here is to decide the deal on a single throw of the dice. It's all or nothing. You're tired of bargaining. Either the sellers accept what you've offered or you'll go elsewhere.

I've personally used this technique many times and it works for me more often than it fails! You just have to be prepared to give up the house in case the sellers remain adamant. For more tips and traps on bargaining, look into my book *Tips and Traps When Negotiating Real Estate* (McGraw-Hill, 1995).

11 Where to Get the Best Financing

Today as never before, you have an excellent chance of getting financing on the property you want. This doesn't mean that you can finance a $1 million home on a $100 paycheck. It does mean, however, that lenders are making it easier than ever to get financing.

One of the newest and most important developments in real estate lending has to do with less qualified buyers. In the past, in order to get a low-down mortgage, you had to be a premium buyer—high salary, few other debts, and sterling credit. Not so anymore. Lenders are taking less qualified buyers and offering them financing with slightly higher interest rates to make up for the added risk. In other words, if you've been shy of applying for a mortgage because of some credit problems, give it a try. You could be surprised at the positive results.

In this chapter we're going to look at the many different types of home mortgages available and where to find the best of them.

Should I Hunt for the Lowest Interest Rate?

For most people, the first consideration with regard to a mortgage is the interest rate. Higher interest rates translate into higher payments; lower rates, lower payments. Consequently, most people want the lowest interest rates possible.

TRAP

Don't hunt for a mortgage only by interest rates. Some mortgages, such as adjustables (discussed shortly), begin with a very low "teaser" interest rate that quickly (within months) climbs higher than that of other mortgages. Shopping by interest rate alone is a fool's game.

TIP

If you have a credit blemish or have trouble otherwise qualifying, shop for a lender, not an interest rate.

The best way to compare interest rates is to do it for *like-kind* mortgages. You don't want to compare apples and oranges.

Today there are two major kinds of conventional (nongovernment insured or guaranteed) mortgages available. With a fixed-rate mortgage, the interest rate does not change for the life of the loan; with an adjustable-rate mortgage, the interest rate changes on a prearranged schedule. When you compare mortgages, be sure you compare fixed-rate to fixed-rate and adjustable to adjustable. (There are so many different varieties of variable-rate mortgages that comparing them is really very difficult.) Of course, at some point, you'll also want to compare adjustable with fixed, but that's a much more complex calculation, as we'll see shortly.

Comparing Fixed-Rate Mortgages

Each lender who offers fixed-rate mortgages posts the current interest rate. These rates are often printed weekly in local papers. Also in many areas a newsletter service gathers them all up and sends them off to brokers. Thus, you can usually find the rates for all the local lenders with one stop at your agent's office.

Here's what a typical list might look like:

Lender's Fixed-Rate Mortgages

ABC S&L	7.5 + 1 + 400
Amalgamated Bank	7.3 + 1.5 + 350
Jones Mortgage Bankers	7.0 + 2.5 + 700
Associated Lenders	7.25 + 2 + 100
WW S&L	7.87 + 0 + 300

At first glance, this list of interest rates might seem fairly complex. What, after all, are all those pluses for? Isn't interest just interest?

Not really. In addition to the actual interest rate to be charged over the life of the mortgage, nearly all lenders of fixed-rate mortgages also charge points and "up-front fees."

Points

A point is a single percentage of a mortgage. Thus 2 points on a $100,000 loan equals $2000, 4 points equals $4000, and so forth.

Points are an additional charge you must pay at the time you secure the mortgages. Thus, if your mortgage is for $100,000 and 2 points, the lender actually funds only $98,000. You must come up with the difference ($2000) in cash yourself at closing.

Points are the lender's way of discounting the mortgage. Yes, the interest rate may say 7.5 percent. But if the mortgage has 2 points, the true interest rate is closer to 8 percent—as revealed on the APR (annual percentage rate) statement that must be given to you.

Why not simply ask a higher interest rate and forget the points? That would be too simple and logical. Lenders prefer to play games with mortgages and borrowers, sticking to an older and arcane system that uses discounts to make it appear that the interest rates are really lower than they are.

Loan Fees

A second charge is an up-front cost often called a "loan fee." This is typically expressed in terms of dollars and may be anywhere from $100 to $700 or more. It is used to cover the lender's costs in preparing the mortgage documents, setting up the repayment account, and executing other bookkeeping functions.

TIP

In the old days there were no "loan fees." Rather, the lender absorbed these costs from the interest payment. Today, however, most loans are sold on a secondary market to government organizations such as Fannie Mae and Freddie Mac, and there is little room for such absorption. Thus, the fees. You can argue with them, but unless they are unreasonable (see Chapter 12), you're stuck with them.

What's the Best Combination of Interest Rate, Points, and Fees?

If you are primarily interested in the lowest monthly payment and have some cash on hand, look for the lowest interest rates. However, be aware that lenders with low interest rates make up for it by jacking up the points.

If you want to reduce your closing costs and can stand a bit higher monthly payment, look for low points. However, often a lender with low points will charge a higher interest rate.

In all cases, ask the lender what the loan fees will be. The lender must disclose these to you. If they are unreasonably high, seek another lender.

TIP

Usually there is no correlation between interest rates and points and loan fees—lenders with high loan fees are just as likely to offer a high interest rate and high points.

Ultimately, you want the *lowest combination* of all three: interest rate, points, and loan fees.

You can get fixed-rate mortgages (both conforming and non-conforming, as covered in Chapter 4) from banks, savings and loans, and mortgage brokers.

How Do I Compare Adjustable-Rate Mortgages?

Adjustable-rate mortgages (ARMs) are also given, except that many more factors are included. Usually the interest rates will seem much lower than for a fixed-rate loan, but don't be fooled. Remember, compare apples with apples, not with oranges.

The low initial interest rate is the appeal of ARMs. As such, they appear to be giving you a better deal. But it ain't necessarily so. There are a number of different factors to take into account with an adjustable-rate mortgage. We'll cover the following in detail:

Teaser rate

Caps

Indices

Margin

Adjustment period

Steps

Teaser Rate

Most ARMs are discounted. This means that the rate at which you initially get the loan is only a "teaser," a come-on to get you to sign up for the ARM. Often they are several percentage points below the true rate. What this means is that in the first few adjustment periods, your effective interest rate will rise even if interest rates in general do not!

As an example, the discounted rate may be 6 percent and the true rate may be 8. You get the ARM at 6 percent. However, it has 3-month adjustment periods with a maximum adjustment of 1 percent in interest each period. Thus, if the interest rate in general does not change, your interest rate automatically will go up 1 percent the first 3 months and 1 percent the second 3 months, so that 6 months after you get the loan you are paying 8 percent instead of 6.

TRAP

Remember, the teaser rate is only temporary. Don't be fooled into thinking that it is the true rate of your mortgage. Ask the lender what the true rate is. You'll be shown the APR (annual percentage rate), which will be higher than the teaser but probably still not as high as the current market rate of the mortgage (because the APR is a blending of the teaser and the current mortgage rate).

Caps

Adjustable rates often have caps, or the maximum amount that the interest rate can rise over the term of the loan and the adjustment period. For example, a summary of different lenders might look like this.

	Interest rate	Cap	Adjustment
AVD S&L	5 + 1	5	6 months
Mary's Bank	4.5 + 2	6/1	3 months
City S&L	3.78 + 1	8	monthly

The interest rates we've already gone over. The cap means the maximum amount the interest rate can rise during the loan period. For AVD S&L, for example, the interest rate can rise a maximum of 5 percent (from the current 5 to 10 percent). For Mary's bank the rate can rise a maximum of 6 percent (from the current 4.5 to 10.5 percent). Mary's bank has a second figure (/1) which indicates that it also has a "payment cap." In other words, regardless of how high the interest rate cap may go, your payments can't rise more than 1 percent (in this case) per adjustment period.

TRAP

Payment caps sound like a good deal, but in reality they are a trap. The problem is that they often lead to "negative amortization," which, simply put, means that you end up owing much more than you originally borrowed!

This happens when the interest rate goes up and your monthly payment does not. In this case, each month you may not be paying enough to meet just the interest on the mortgage, let alone repaying the principal. The excess interest is then added to the principal and you end up paying more than you originally borrowed! (Usually the lender cannot increase the principal of the mortgage over 125 percent of its original amount through negative amortization.)

Generally you want to avoid payment caps and look for the lowest interest rate cap. The lower the cap, the less the interest rate can rise during the term of the mortgage.

TIP

You need to worry about negative amortization only if you have a cap on the payment of your mortgage. If you have no payment cap (assuming a normal loan), you don't have negative amortization.

TIP

Generally speaking, look for the longest adjustment period possible. This will give you more time between monthly payment changes (although when they do come, they can be more dramatic).

Indices

Adjustable-rate mortgages are all geared to different indices. These indices rise and fall along with other interest rates and, accordingly, so does the rate on your mortgage. Ideally, you want an interest rate which has the least volatility. On the other hand, frequently the lender wants a more volatile interest rate to protect money that has been loaned.

The most commonly used indices include:

1. 6-month T-bill rate
2. 1-year T-bill rate
3. 3-year T-bill rate
4. Libor index (London Interbranch rate)
5. Cost of funds for the lender
6. Average of fixed-rate mortgages
7. Average rate paid on jumbo CDs

TIP

Historically the two lowest rates have been the cost of funds and the Libor index. However, as we move into new economic climates, that could change. Lenders will provide you with a chart showing changes in the index for your loan. Be sure you ask for a chart that includes the period of 1979 through 1981 and 1989 to 1995 so you can see how the index performed in high-interest-rate and low-interest-rate economic conditions.

Margin

Each adjustable rate has a margin. This is a figure that is added to the index to give you your interest rate. For example, the margin might be 3 percent. Thus, if the index is at 5 percent, add the 3 percent margin and you have your effective interest rate of 8 percent.

TRAP

Keep in mind that the index rate is not your interest rate. Typically the lender's margin is added to the index, this can increase your effective interest rate by 2 to 5 percent.

TIP

You want as low a margin as possible. The lower the margin, the lower your interest rate.

Adjustment Period

The adjustment period is the length of time between interest rate changes on your loan. As noted, it can vary enormously. The more frequent the adjustment period, the more volatile your mortgage payments. The longer the adjustment period, the more stable your monthly payments. In a market with rising interest rates, it is to your advantage to get the longest adjustment periods possible so that your mortgage remains stable. When interest rates are falling, you'll get the benefit sooner with shorter adjustment periods.

Steps

Steps refer to how high the mortgage interest can be raised in any given adjustment period. An ARM with 2-point steps means that in any period, the interest rate can be raised as much as 2 percent, dramatically affecting your payment. (Usually hikes this high are found only in a high-interest-rate market, or when the teaser rate is being brought up to market level.) Usually you will want a mortgage with the smallest steps possible.

Comparing adjustable-rate mortgages can be tricky. In addition to the interest rate and points, you have to compare all the other factors we've discussed previously. Here are some guidelines that should prove helpful.

TIP

If you're going to live in the home only a short time and then sell, get the lowest teaser rate with the longest adjustment periods and shortest steps possible. For example, if you plan to live in the property for only 3 years, you might be able to find an ARM that gives you a below-market interest rate for the entire period of time!

TIP

Most people aim for the most stable index. That way you have a better idea of your monthly payments. But if interest rates are falling, you may want a more volatile index that will reflect falling rates in a falling monthly payment.

TIP

Don't compare just interest rates and points. Sometimes an ARM with a higher interest rate and more points is a better deal, if it has a more favorable adjustment period, steps, margin, and so on.

TIP

Some mortgage brokers will give you a computer breakdown of different ARMs with comparisons based on the factors you are most concerned about. These can be very helpful when comparing different adjustable mortgages.

TRAP

Stay away from payment caps that result in negative amortization. Stay away from very short adjustment periods (1 month). Beware of very low teaser rates—usually there's something else in the mortgage you really won't like.

Adjustable-rate mortgages are available from banks, savings and loans, and mortgage brokers.

How Do I Compare Adjustable-Rate and Fixed-Rate Mortgages?

Now we're at the stage of comparing apples with oranges. In truth, a direct one-to-one comparison just isn't very helpful. Rather, what's more important to most borrowers is comparing the usefulness of each type. It's sort of like saying, "Do I want to eat an orange now, or will an apple taste better?"

Here are some guidelines that may prove helpful.

TIP

When interest rates are low, get a fixed-rate mortgage and lock in the low rate. When interest rates are high, consider an adjustable-rate mortgage with payments that will fall as interest rates come down.

TIP

If you desperately want to buy a home but can't qualify for a fixed-rate mortgage, try an adjustable. The lower teaser rate should make qualifying a bit easier. (Currently lenders qualify not just on the basis of the teaser, but on an average between the market rate and the teaser, which is still probably lower than for a comparable fixed-rate mortgage.)

TIP

If you can't afford to have fluctuations in your monthly payment, get a fixed-rate mortgage. You'll at least know what your payments will be every month.

TIP

If you plan to sell soon, get an ARM and take advantage of the low teaser rate. But beware, your plans could change unexpectedly!

TIP

Sometimes ARMs have lower initial loan costs. If cash is a big consideration for you, look into them.

TRAP

Remember that with an ARM, if interest rates go up, so do your payments. (This may occur even after rates have peaked and started to come down. Because of your adjustment period, you may play "catch-up" for months after the downturn.) You can't call your lender later and say, "I can't handle a $200 increase in my monthly payment!" Your lender isn't going to be sympathetic and will threaten you with foreclosure if you don't pay. The time to consider a big monthly increase is before you get that adjustable-rate mortgage, not afterward.

What About a Combination Fixed and Adjustable Mortgage?

There are a whole bunch of hybrids out there, any one of which may be better for your situation than a straight fixed or ARM mortgage.

Convertible Mortgage

Some ARMs may be "convertible" to a fixed rate. Many allow a conversion at a set date—3 or 7 years, for example—in the future. Just be sure the conversion is guaranteed at the lowest interest rate at the time of conversion.

There are literally hundreds of types of convertible mortgages available. Some lenders will even create one just to suit your financial situation. Be sure to ask.

Short-Term Fixed, Amortized over 30 Years

The whole point behind an ARM, from a lender's perspective, is to give a loan that can respond to interest rate fluctuations. Another way of accomplishing this is to give a shorter-term fixed-rate mortgage. Currently lenders are offering short-term fixed-rate mortgages in the following time lengths, all amortized over 30 years:

15 years
10 years
7 years
5 years
3 years

The shorter the term, the better the interest rate is. For example, you can get an interest rate reduction if you agree to pay off your mortgage in 15 years instead of 30. If you agree to pay it off in 3, you might get the interest rate reduced by a full percentage point or more! (*Note:* The monthly payments are still amortized on the basis of 30 years. It's just that you have a shorter due date, or balloon payment at the end.)

TRAP

Beware of very short-term fixed-rate mortgages. If it turns out that you can't sell or refinance as you planned at the end of the term, you could lose the property to foreclosure! You're gambling a lower interest rate on future market and personal financial conditions.

TIP

Make sure a shorter-term mortgage includes an automatic refinancing option at the end. Usually this is an ugly adjustable, but at least if worse comes to worst, you won't be without a loan.

Hybrid mortgages are also available from banks, savings and loans, and mortgage brokers. However, you best sources are the mortgage brokers, who deal with many lenders and, thus, have a better sense of what's out there.

What About a Fully Amortized 15-Year Mortgage?

As opposed to the hybrids just discussed, in a fully amortized mortgage, the payments are higher so it can be fully paid off at the end of 15 years. (With a hybrid, you have lower payments, but a balloon at the end.)

The advantage here is less interest. With a 30-year mortgage the total interest is more than twice as much at the same interest rate than with a 15-year mortgage! Of course, you may be saying to yourself that this is all well and good—yes, you save more than half the interest. But you probably more than double your payments.

Not at all. The difference in payments between the same 15-year and 30-year mortgages is only about 20 percent. You'll end up paying only about 20 percent more monthly. (Yes, it really does work out that way. It's all in the way mortgages are calculated.)

TRAP

From the above discussion, the most likely conclusion to jump to is to get a 15-year mortgage—look at all the interest saved. The problem is the 15 percent higher monthly payment. What if during the time you're paying back the mortgage, you get ill or lose your job? It's a lot harder to repay a higher monthly payment than a lower one. The solution is to get a 30-year mortgage with no prepayment penalty. (Many modern mortgages don't have penalties for early repayment.) No prepayment penalty means that you can repay more than your monthly payment at any time. Then, instead of paying the regular monthly payment, voluntarily pay an extra 15 percent each month. You'll now pay off the mortgage in roughly half the time, 15 years. In addition, if you ever get into any trouble, you can fall back and repay at the lower required payment. It's just some added insurance for you.

What About Biweekly Payments?

Popular a few years ago, some biweekly mortgages are still around. Here, instead of paying your mortgage each month, you pay half the monthly amount every other week. The result is that you actually pay an extra month each year. (There are 12 months, but 52 weeks in a year, meaning you would make 26 biweekly payments.) Over the long haul, that extra month means you end up paying more in principal each year, which means much less interest down the road. This works for either a 30-year or a 15-year mortgage.

TIP

The problem with biweekly mortgages is that you can be forever writing checks. Therefore, the only realistic way of handling them is to have the money taken out of your account automatically every 2 weeks.

TRAP

The biweekly mortgage is not for someone who is self-employed and gets paid irregularly. An unstable cashflow can cause real problems when you have a mortgage payment due every other week.

What About Getting a Government Mortgage?

The government, except in some rare instances, does not lend mortgage money. It does, however, insure or guarantee lenders, who thus are willing to make you better than conventional (nongovernment) mortgages.

FHA Program

FHA mortgages are insured by the government and are offered by most lenders, such as banks and S&Ls. Generally the interest rate is a bit lower, although the points can be higher. The problem is that the ceiling, or maximum rate, for FHA loans is relatively low.

TRAP

If you get a new FHA loan, you'll have to pay the insurance premium for the loan up front. The premium is fairly high—close to 4 percent of the loan amount. You can, however, add the premium to the loan, although this does increase your monthly payments. Additionally, you are required to occupy the property as your residence, and the property itself must pass a strict qualifying appraisal.

TRAP

There are generally no prepayment penalties for FHA mortgages and they are partially assumable. (That means that the buyers must qualify as if they were getting a new FHA loan. However, generally they can assume the sellers' loan at the existing interest rate.)

Veterans Program

Some loans are guaranteed by the Veterans Administration. The guarantee is not to you, but to the bank or S&L that makes the loan. These mortgages offer competitive interest rates and, in many cases, no down payments and reduced costs.

In order to get a VA loan you must have been on the active list in the armed forces during certain periods of time. (These change periodically—check with the Veterans Administration for the current requirements.) In addition, the property must pass a rigorous appraisal. Finally, you must plan to occupy the property.

TIP

VA loans are usually nothing down to you and the seller must pay most of the closing costs. Further, in general, they are fully assumable. You can sell the property and the buyers can pick up the loan at the existing interest rate.

TRAP

Once you get a VA loan, you are on the hook for that loan for as long as it is on the property. Even if at some later date you sell the property, you may still be responsible for the loan! If the future buyer defaults, the VA could come looking to you for repayment! You must get a release of responsibility from the VA at the time someone else buys to fully get off the hook. (But that next buyer must then qualify as a veteran.)

Can I Get a Graduated-Payment Loan?

Less popular today than in the past, loans with a graduated (instead of fixed) payment can be incorporated with almost any other, including government loans. Generally it means that you pay less when you first get the loan and are least able to pay. Then, presumably as your income goes up, so does the monthly payment.

TRAP

Don't get a graduated-payment loan unless you're quite certain you're going to have an increase in income. If your income remains the same or declines, you could be in big trouble down the road.

What About Reverse-Equity (Annuity) Mortgages?

After a halting start over a decade ago, reverse-equity mortgages are making a comeback. Designed for senior citizens, they allow you to live in your paid-off house and get a monthly stipend. The amount that you receive is added to a mortgage. You can stay in the house until you die; then the lender gets the place and can resell.

TIP

Be sure the loan provides that you can live in the property in perpetuity. You wouldn't want to be evicted after a dozen years or so because the mortgage had grown higher than the value of the property. Check out this feature in an FHA version.

Very few lenders offer reverse-equity loans. Consult with a mortgage broker about possible sources in your area.

Should I Ask the Sellers for a Second Mortgage?

If the sellers are willing, it's probably the best mortgage you can get. There's usually no qualifying and you can bargain for the interest rate. (You might offer a slightly higher purchase price for a lower interest rate.)

Many sellers, however, cannot give a second mortgage because they need to cash out in order to buy another home. Others are reluctant, fearing you might not make the payments and they would have the considerable expense of foreclosing and taking the property back.

You can also get a second mortgage from an institutional lender such as a bank. Here the second mortgage typically has a higher interest rate than the first.

TRAP

Beware of "balloon payments" on seconds. This results when the mortgage is not fully amortized—when the monthly payments do not fully pay off the principal. At the end of the term, you could end up owing a substantial amount of money. For example, if you borrow $10,000 at 10 percent, interest only, for 7 years, at the end of the term, you still owe $10,000! (Remember, the mortgage was for "interest only," meaning that the monthly payments covered only the interest.)

Some seconds have payments which only partially return all the principal. This is frequently the case with a mortgage that is "amortized for 15 years, due in 5." That means that the monthly payment is high enough to pay back the loan in 15 years. But you owe it all back in 5 years. When the fifth year comes around, most of your principal is still owing. Now you must either dig deep into your pockets or refinance.

What Are Discount/Prepayment Mortgages?

Just recently entering the market, discount/prepayment loans offer a discount on the interest rate or points or both, provided you agree not to pay off (prepay) the mortgage for a set period of time. For example, the lender may offer you a $2500 discount provided you won't prepay within 3 years.

If for whatever reason you must prepay before the time limit, you are subject to a hefty penalty, sometimes 6 months' worth of interest.

TIP

This is great, provided you don't have to suddenly refinance or sell. If you do, the penalty could kill you.

TRAP

Beware of lenders who offer a very low incentive discount, a very long prepayment period, and a high penalty. You could end up being locked in for 5 years just to save $500 bucks, with thousands in penalties for prepaying.

Discount/prepayment loans are available from banks, savings and loans, and mortgage brokers on most types of mortgages, including both fixed and adjustable.

12
Can You Cut Your Closing Costs?

Closing costs tend to be a surprise. Most buyers worry about finding enough cash for the down and coming up with monthly payments; they seldom worry about closing costs. But then, that's only natural. Almost anytime we buy anything in the store, there are closing costs in the form of sales tax, delivery charges, or other fees. Most of us just assume that there will be some additional, though minimal, charges for any transaction.

The trouble is that closing costs for the home buyer can be substantial. Depending on the transaction, they can even be as much or more than the down payment!

All of which is to say that one of the best ways of reducing your home purchase expense is by cutting your closing costs to the bare minimum. That's what we'll see how to do in this chapter.

Aren't Closing Costs Regulated?

Yes and no. RESPA (Real Estate Settlement Procedures Act) specifies that a lender must give you a good-faith estimate of what your costs for the loan, and in effect the transaction, will be within 3 days of your making a formal application. Giving you notice, however, does not necessarily mean reducing those costs. The lender can merely inform you that the costs are going to be exceedingly high.

TIP

The real advantage of having a good-faith estimate early on from a lender is that if the costs are too high, you have time shop for a loan elsewhere.

In addition, any good real estate agent will give you an estimate of your closing costs, often before you make your offer and certainly right after. One excellent real estate agent I know claims that she has never been more than $25 off in her estimates, and she closes several dozen deals a year!

Nevertheless, it behooves every buyer to examine what the closing costs might be to see where they can be reduced. Here's a list of typical closing costs when purchasing a home. (*Note:* You probably won't have all of these; you may have most of them.)

Typical Closing Costs

- Insurance

  Policy of fire insurance
  Homeowner's insurance
  Home warranty package

- Taxes

  Prorations
  Tax service contract

- Mortgage

  Assumption fee
  Document preparation fee
  Loan fee
  Account setup fee
  Impound setup/service fee
  IRS filing fee
  Attorney fee
  Collection setup fee

- Attorney

  Document preparation fee
  Services rendered fee

- Recording

  Deed
  Affidavit of value
  Encumbrance (or release of)
  Assumption

- Escrow

  Document preparation fee
  Escrow fee
  Interest proration
  Taxes proration
  Rents proration
  Insurance proration

- Title Insurance

  Title insurance fee
  ALTA fee
  Other fee

What should be fairly obvious after looking at the various potential fees that you could be charged for closing costs is that there's a lot of them, and for the average person, they seem written in a foreign language. After all, what's an "ALTA" fee or an "impound setup/service fee" or any of the dozens of other fees? Are they all legitimate? How much should you expect to pay? Let's go over them one at a time.

Why Do I Have to Pay for Insurance?

As the buyer of a home (new or resale) you will want to carry fire insurance. This insures you, and the lender, that in the event of a catastrophe, the home can be rebuilt.

TRAP

Don't think you can save money by just taking a chance and just not insuring the property. The lender will demand that you carry minimum fire insurance as a condition of the financing. If you don't, the lender will put its own, usually more expensive policy on the property and bill you for it. If you refuse to pay, you could be placed in default and the lender could foreclose.

While you are required to pay for fire and basic hazard insurance, you are not usually required to carry a "homeowner's policy" (although some lenders do now require it). The homeowner's policy runs almost twice as much as the basic fire/hazard policy, but it's a good investment. It protects you against a wide variety of losses, including liability if someone gets hurt on your property.

A home warranty package (discussed in Chapter 8) is optional. It typically costs from $250 upward annually, depending on the quality of coverage. It's also a good idea.

TIP

A home warranty package protects the sellers as much as you. If something physically goes wrong with the property's various water, electrical, heating, and cooling systems, chances are you'll be angry at the sellers and demand they pay for it. With the home warranty package, it's all taken care of. Therefore, insist that the seller pay for it. In many cases, the seller will.

Do I Have to Pay Taxes on the Purchase?

It's the only thing that's certain, besides death. You do not have to pay sales tax (at least not yet!), although some states do charge a usually nominal "transfer tax." But you will have to pay property taxes. The escrow company prorates your share of the year's taxes. (See an explanation of proration in Chapter 8.)

If you are getting a new loan that does not have a tax impound account, the lender may also require that you pay for a "tax service contract." The fee is usually around $25 to $50. What this contract does is hire a company to watch your property's tax records. If you fail to pay them, a report is sent to the lender, who then pays the taxes, adds the amount onto your mortgage, and often begins foreclosure.

What Are the Mortgage Closing Costs?

If you get a new mortgage, you're going to have to pay closing costs on it. This is usually the most costly area for the buyer. Often the costs of closing the mortgage can come to 2 or 3 percent or more of the total amount. Here are the fees and what they should be.

Assumption Fee

If you're assuming an existing mortgage, you have to pay a fee. It's typically in the $100 or less range.

TRAP

Most fixed-rate mortgages are not assumable, so you probably won't have (or shouldn't have) an assumption charge. They are written with "due on sale" or "alienation" clauses which prevent you from assuming them. Today the only really assumable mortgages are FHA-insured and VA-guaranteed loans and even these may have qualifying conditions. Some ARMs (adjustable rate mortgages) are quasi-assumable. That means that you can assume the indebtedness, but the interest rate is often hiked up to the current market rate and you may have to go through a qualifying process similar to that of any new loan. Don't be misled into believing you can automatically assume a mortgage.

Document Preparation Fee

A nonsense fee must be paid to the lender for preparing the loan documents. Since the lender is making the loan and since it takes only a few taps on a computer keyboard to spit out the documents, it's absurd to charge a high fee for it. Up to $50 is more than reasonable, but fees can go as high as $500 or more. Anything over $50 and you're being ripped off.

TIP

You can refuse to pay a preparation fee. The lender, however, can refuse to fund the loan, so in the end you may have to pay it anyway. The best thing to do is to read carefully your good-faith estimate of fees to find out in advance (before you secure financing) if the lender has a document fee and how much it is. At that time, you can more easily walk away and find a new lender.

Points

A point is equal to 1 percent of the mortgage. If the mortgage is for $100,000, 2 points is equal to $2000.

Lenders charge points for a variety of reasons, usually to offset a lower-than-market interest rate that you may be getting. The amount of points you pay varies according to the market. I've seen points as high as 10 and as low as zero. Be sure you shop around before you secure financing from the lender offering the lowest points. (See Chapter 11.)

TIP

The points you pay to get a home loan are usually considered interest and may be deducted from your annual income tax. The rule for this, however, seems to change frequently, so check with your tax accountant to see how much, if any, may be deductible.

Loan Fee

The loan fee is an up-front charge in addition to points. Many lenders, for example, will charge "2 points plus $400." The $400 is the loan fee and usually goes to cover such work as preparing documents and funding the money. Of course, it's preposterous to pay points as well as a loan fee and document preparation fee. A good lender will not charge these, or charge only a minimal loan fee. All the costs will be up front, where you can see them in the points.

TRAP

Remember, if you wait until escrow is ready to close to complain, it's too late. To avoid this, you must get a good lender and negotiate the loan fee at the time you apply for financing.

Account Setup Fee

Some lenders may charge you to set up the payback account, the little payment book or monthly invoices you'll get when you pay. This is another absurd fee.

Determine well in advance the charges your lender will make and negotiate them down.

Impound Account and Setup/Service Fee

Some loans require you to pay one-twelfth of your taxes and insurance each month. "Impound" simply means the holding of tax and insurance money for you (and then paying it out appropriately.) Recent legislation has required lenders to be more scrupulous as to how they handle impound accounts and to demand only a minimum amount of money, usually no more than a month or two, for the account.

Many lenders, however, will charge you for setting up this account. Again, this is a ridiculous charge, since it's the lender who insists on having the impound account.

Attorney Fee

You may also have to pay a fee to the lender's attorney (not yours, which we'll cover later) for checking over the mortgage documents and the transaction. It's another ripoff. Unless the deal is unusual in some way, the lender should have attorneys on staff (virtually all do) who automatically check documents and deals. It should be part of the lending service, not a separate charge.

TIP

I would refuse to pay the attorney fee. But I would refuse at the time I applied for the loan and negotiate it out with the lender.

Collection Setup Fee

A collection setup fee is usually charged if part of the property is a rental and rents need to be collected and paid directly to the lender, or if your payment is going to be paid directly out of your paycheck or checking account to the lender.

This fee is atypical and shouldn't appear unless the lender discusses special circumstances with you in advance.

What About My Attorney's Fees?

You will probably want to have an attorney representing you. The attorney should interact at various stages during the transaction. An important appearance should be at closing, to explain the various documents you will be asked to sign as well as the various closing costs noted here.

One of those closing costs will be the attorney fee. This may be a single fee or may be broken down into several areas such as document preparation, legal advice, services rendered, and so forth.

TIP

The attorneys who work in real estate usually have set fees for standard transactions. These fees are normally between $500 and $1000. Be sure you discuss the fees before hiring an attorney. Remember, the attorney fees, like everything else, are negotiable.

What Are Recording Fees?

The escrow company charges fees for recording documents. The typical cost is $7 to $12 per document. If the fees are any higher than this, be sure to ask for an explanation.

Why Are There Escrow Costs?

Assuming that you are using an independent escrow company (and you certainly should), there will be a separate charge. The cost usually varies according to the price of the house. A minimum of $250 to $300 is often the case.

TIP

Usually the party (buyer or seller) who pays for the escrow costs is determined by custom in the particular area. Sometimes it is customary to split these costs with the seller. Other times, either the seller or the buyer pays all of them. You will be pressured to follow custom for your area. You don't have to, however. (See below on having the seller pay your costs.)

As part of the escrow charges there may also be other prorations of interest, taxes, rents, and insurance. Just be sure that you're paying only your fair share.

TRAP

Items typically are prorated at the close of escrow. However, if you are not getting possession of the property until a later date (probably a bad idea; see Chapter 8), then it's unfair for you to have to pay interest, insurance, and taxes until that date. If you're taking possession later than the close of escrow, be sure that prorations are made as of that later date.

Do I Really Need Title Insurance?

No lender will offer a mortgage without title insurance. Even if by some miracle you should find one who did, you shouldn't ever buy a property without title insurance. It is what guarantees that you actually have what you purchased.

The cost of title insurance varies according to the price of the property. A $100,000 property might cost you anywhere from $300 to $600, depending on the area of the country and the title insurance company.

TIP

There are lots of title insurance companies. Typically the escrow company or the agents will prefer a specific company. That may be because the title company is giving them perks or because the real estate agency owns the title company. (Perks might be something as innocuous as free stationery to something as serious as free vacations.) The relationship between the title company and the agent should be disclosed to you. Since for practical purposes one title company is as good as another, it really shouldn't matter to you—except in the case of fees. If one title company is cheaper than another, I would insist on the cheaper company. You must do this at the time escrow is opened.

A standard policy of title insurance protects you. However, lenders will often insist on your obtaining additional insurance called an ALTA (American Land Title Association) policy. It gives the lender additional assurances, often including an inspection of the property. (In some states the ALTA has a different name. In California, for example, a CLTA [California Land Title Association] policy is usually accepted in lieu of an ALTA policy.)

TIP

Usually the seller pays for the standard policy guaranteeing you clear title, although custom in some areas dictates that the costs are split or that the buyer pays.

> You, however, usually must always pay for the additional ALTA policy. Again, who pays is negotiable, although it's rare for a seller to pay for an ALTA policy.

These, then, are the typical closing costs you will encounter. Now, how do you get them lowered?

There are two ways, both of which have already been suggested. First, know what the costs and fees should be. If a fee is unreasonable or a cost excessive, demand it be eliminated or changed. Usually you are dealing with a lender and if you make your demand at the time you are first applying for the loan, you have the leverage. Remember, you can always walk away. (Your leverage will depend to some extent on market conditions: When there is high demand for mortgages, you'll have less leverage; when demand is low, you'll have more.)

The second method is to insist that the seller pay part or all of your closing costs. This must be done at the time you make your offer and should be written into the sales agreement.

Why would a seller pay your costs?

Perhaps you're giving that seller a better price than he or she anticipated, or better terms. In a trade-off, the seller pays your closing costs.

Why would you offer better price or terms? Perhaps you're cash-short. Remember, the closing costs are cash, while 90 percent or more of the purchase price can be financed. You offer the seller a higher price (assuming the property appraises out), and the seller pays your cash closing costs. You don't need to come up with as much cash.

Of course, some buyers who are very tough negotiators argue for it all—good price, good terms, and seller pays closing costs! In a bad market where houses just aren't selling, sometimes desperate sellers will agree.

13
How Do I Inspect the House?

Should you have a home inspection as part of your purchase?

Yes, absolutely, and the sale should be contingent upon your approval of the inspection.

Should you do the inspection yourself?

Yes, absolutely.

Should you also hire a professional?

Yes, absolutely. Go along with the professional inspector so that the two of you do the inspection.

You need to have good, detailed information on the condition of the home you are buying. After all, just because it's standing today doesn't mean that it isn't ready to fall over tomorrow.

In the past, the dictum "Let the buyer beware!" was the rule in house hunting. Today, however, consumerism has turned the tables. Today it's "Let the seller beware." Sellers in many areas of the country must present to you, the buyer, a disclosure listing any and all faults with the house, often at the time you first see it or at least at the time you make a purchase offer. (In California, for example, you have 3 days to evaluate the disclosure statement. If you're given the disclosure after the seller has accepted your offer, you may have grounds for backing out of the deal for up to 3 days.)

Further, sellers now expect a buyer to insist on a home inspection. After all, it protects the seller, in many cases, even more than you! The reason is that while sellers may know many of the home's problems (such as a leaky roof or broken window), they may know next to nothing about the house's heating system or its foundation. For that reason, many sellers are glad to have an inspector's report to go along with their disclosure statement. It shows they have diligently made an effort to learn about problems and disclose them.

TIP

Expect the seller to pay for your home inspection, probably around $250 to $350. Remember, it protects the seller as well, maybe more.

The time to insist on a home inspection is when you make your initial offer. Write it into the sales agreement. Make sure that it's a contingency. (See Chapter 8 for a description of contingency clauses.)

TRAP

Sellers are no fools. Yes, they are almost universally prepared to let you have a home inspection. But they won't let you tie up their property indefinitely. Typically they will limit your inspection contingency by insisting that it be completed and your approval given within 7 or perhaps 10 days. If you don't approve, the deal's off and the house is back on the market. Indeed, many sellers will insist that they be able to continue showing the house and to accept backup offers until you remove the inspection contingency.

Where Do I Find a Home Inspector?

Ask your real estate agent. Usually active agents know of several they can recommend. Ask the lender or the escrow officer. As a last resort, try the phone book.

When you select an inspector, ask if he or she is a member of ASHI (American Society of Home Inspectors) or NAHI (National Association of Home Inspectors). It doesn't guarantee competence, but it indicates they at least belong to national trade associations.

TRAP

At this point home inspectors are not yet licensed in most states. That means that anyone—you, I, or the guy who sold you this book—can hang out a shingle and be an inspector. That means it's up to you to be sure you're dealing with someone competent.

Ask your future inspector for at least three referrals from past jobs. Then call those people. Hopefully, it will be at least 6 months or more since the inspection and they will have had an opportunity to see if something came up that wasn't initially discovered. You may get some surprising answers.

Check the inspector's credentials: What qualifies him or her to be an inspector? Look for someone with a related degree and a broad building background such as a soils or building engineer. Often retired county or city building inspectors make great choices.

TRAP

Many former contractors make money on the side as inspectors. That's okay, but just because a person has a contractor's license doesn't mean he or she knows anything about a home inspection. A plumbing contractor, for example, may be able to do a great job checking out your sinks and toilets. But the contractor may know next to nothing about the wiring.

Why Should I Go Along on the Inspection?

It's the only way you can really learn what the home's problems are. An inspection is both oral and written. In the oral part, the inspector describes problems to you as you go through, under, and over the home. You can ask questions and can often get useful information on how to correct a problem as well as how much that correction will cost.

A written report, on the other hand, is often more formal. These days many inspectors are afraid to write down any but the most glaring of problems for fear that they could be sued by the seller for exaggerating something. Hence, the written reports tend to be bland and, quite frankly, not that useful. Often they are filled with more disclaimers than information. That's why you need to go along and listen to what the inspector says.

What Should I Look For?

The inspector will point things out. But your inspector might not be the best in the world, so you should have an idea what to look for yourself. Below is a home inspection checklist. Use it as a guide either with an inspector or, if you're bolder, when you inspect the property yourself. Keep in mind that while it offers many ideas, it is not complete. There may be problems with the property beyond the scope of the checklist. (Also check out my 1995 book *The Home Inspector's Troubleshooter.*)

TRAP

Don't try doing an inspection on your own unless you know a great deal about buildings. I've been inspecting properties for more than 30 years and I still usually hire an engineer to go along with me. The engineer can point out things that I miss and vice versa.

Home Inspection Checklist

Drainage

Drainage problems can lead to cracked foundations and slabs. They can cause a house to shift, particularly if it's located on a hillside, and in extreme cases can cause the actual collapse of the home.

The correction of drainage problems is best left to experts. However, even a beginner can usually tell where drainage problems exist.

	YES	NO
1. Is there dampness under the house? (The basement should be dry as dust.)	[ ]	[ ]
2. Are there footprints or ribbed patterns in the dirt under the house, indicating that when it rains, water creeps in?	[ ]	[ ]
3. Is there mold (black or green) on wood under the house, indicating heavy moisture?	[ ]	[ ]

	YES	NO
4. Does the ground outside slope *away* from the house? (If it slopes into the house, you've got serious problems.)	[ ]	[ ]

Foundation

The concrete foundation is what supports your house. Usually there is a peripheral foundation which goes around the entire edge of the home. Within this peripheral foundation there may be concrete blocks holding up piers that support the floor (in a wood floor home) or a concrete slab (in a cement floor home).

The peripheral foundation (also called footings) extends upward perhaps half a foot or more from the ground to where the wood frame of the house begins. It also extends downward into the soil. The further down the foundation extends and the wider it is, the better. In areas with expansive soil (the soil swells when wet) or other soil problems, the concrete foundation should be a minimum of 16 inches deep by 8 inches wide. In areas with freezing weather, it may need to go even deeper.

In addition, there should be steel rods in the concrete. The steel holds the concrete together. (Cement by itself will crack easily.)

Cracks in the foundation can lead to uneven floors inside the house. It can also lead to slippage down a hillside as well as to broken windows and cracks appearing in walls and ceilings.

Some breakage of foundations happens naturally over time. However, severe breakage indicates a problem which could get worse.

	YES	NO
1. Do you see cracks in the foundation when you walk around the exterior of the house? (Hairline cracks always occur and should be disregarded.)	[ ]	[ ]
2. Are the cracks wider at the top than at the bottom? (This indicates actual breakage, a serious problem if the top of the break is ¼ inch or more.)	[ ]	[ ]
3. Is there an actual separation in the foundation? (This indicates that not enough steel reinforcement was used when the foundation was built.)	[ ]	[ ]
4. In a slab house, does the floor feel uneven when you walk over it (indicating cracks hidden under carpets or tiles)?	[ ]	[ ]
5. Under a house, do any of the girders sag (a sign that the foundation has slipped)?	[ ]	[ ]

Roof

The purpose of the roof, besides providing an aesthetic look, is to keep rain and snow out of the house. The cost of repairing a roof can be high, of replacing a roof enormous ($5000 to $15,000 or more, as of this writing). You want to be sure that the roof is in good shape. If it's not, you may want to have the seller fix or replace it or make an adjustment to the price.

Some general information on roofs is in order.

Wood shake roofs. Depending on the thickness of the shake, they can last 20 to 30 years. If the house you are buying has a wood shake roof and it's 20 years old or older, check the roof very carefully.

	YES	NO
1. Are there pieces of the roof lying on the ground around the house? (This is an obvious bad sign.)	[ ]	[ ]
2. Using binoculars, can you see missing shingles anywhere on the roof?	[ ]	[ ]
3. Are the shingles intact? (Badly cracked shingles are another bad sign.)	[ ]	[ ]
4. Are there any signs of leakage in the ceiling or walls inside the house? Go into the attic and look up. If it's daytime and you see light pouring through many tiny or large holes, you've got trouble.	[ ]	[ ]

Composition shingles. Made of tar, fiberglass, or some similar composition, they have a lifespan of 15 to 30 years, depending on the quality.

	YES	NO
1. Is the *color* of the shingles good? (Fading shingles are a sure sign of wear.)	[ ]	[ ]
2. Are the edges of the shingles curling up? (This is a sign of wear in hot climates.)	[ ]	[ ]
3. Are there any bare spots on the roof?	[ ]	[ ]
4. Are there any signs of leakage in the ceiling or walls inside the house?	[ ]	[ ]

Aluminum shingles. These have a lifespan of 50 years. Generally they don't wear out unless they have been damaged.

	YES	NO
1. Are there signs of peeling or fading of their color? (The shingles may continue to keep the weather out, but will look terrible.)	[ ]	[ ]

	YES	NO
2. Are there any dents or separations in the shingles, indicating someone has walked on them?	[ ]	[ ]
3. Are there any signs of leakage in the ceiling or walls inside the house?	[ ]	[ ]

Tiles. Tile roofs last indefinitely (80 years or more). However, they can easily be broken, and once broken they lose their ability to keep the weather out. *Don't walk on tile roofs—you'll break the tiles.*

	YES	NO
1. Are any of the tiles broken?	[ ]	[ ]
2. Have any fallen off?	[ ]	[ ]
3. Are there any signs of leakage in the ceiling or walls inside the house?	[ ]	[ ]

Paint

Interior. In a resale, don't expect to get a house that doesn't require repainting. As noted in an earlier chapter, as soon as the seller's furniture gets moved out, you're going to see whole areas that need repainting. The only question is: Will you do it or will the seller?

	YES	NO
1. Are there marks on the walls?	[ ]	[ ]
2. Is the current paint flaking, indicating it will have to be sanded before new paint can be applied?	[ ]	[ ]
3. Are the colors light or dark? (Covering dark colors may require two or more new coats.)	[ ]	[ ]

Exterior. Weathering is the problem here. Even the best paints usually don't last more than 5 to 7 years. Repainting the exterior can be more expensive than painting the interior, since it often requires removing chipped and peeling paint.

	YES	NO
1. Is the paint chipped or peeling?	[ ]	[ ]
2. Are the colors faded? (Faded colors indicate paint that is aging.)	[ ]	[ ]
3. Is the caulking around windows starting to fall out?	[ ]	[ ]
4. Is the aluminum siding becoming detached?	[ ]	[ ]
5. Are the gutters falling?	[ ]	[ ]
6. Is the paint on the gutters peeling?	[ ]	[ ]

Plumbing

In general, you need an expert to tell you if there are serious plumbing problems. There are, however, some telltale signs you can check for.

	YES	NO
1. Is the plumbing galvanized steel? (Galvanized steel lasts about 30 years, sometimes less. Copper lasts virtually forever.)	[ ]	[ ]
2. Are there leaks at the joints of galvanized pipes? (Usually visible under the house or in the garage, leaks indicate that electrolytic action may be corroding the pipes and they could need to be replaced—$5000 or more.)	[ ]	[ ]
3. Are there leaks under the sinks in any of the bathrooms or kitchen? (Possibly a minor problem, but why should you have to fix it?	[ ]	[ ]
4. Is the water heater old? (The date is sometimes stamped on the label—a water heater rarely lasts more than 7 to 10 years.)	[ ]	[ ]
5. Does the water heater have a temperature/pressure safety valve? (This is vitally important. If you're not sure what a safety valve is, have a professional check it out.)	[ ]	[ ]

In addition, the gas supply line needs to be checked. A professional should do this.

Wiring

This is the venue of the professional. Don't attempt to make a judgment on the wiring unless you're an electrician. Some danger signals to watch for include:

	YES	NO
1. Do switches or sockets spark when used?	[ ]	[ ]
2. Are there inoperative lights or switches?	[ ]	[ ]

Heating

Even more so than in the case of wiring, a professional needs to check out the heating. If you're using gas, you need to be sure that there are no leaks. Here are some telltale signs to look for.

	YES	NO
1. Do you smell burned gas fumes coming from heating vents? Does the flame in the furnace turn yellow and rise high above the burners? (These are bad signs indicating a leak in the heat exchanger, a dangerous condition usually requiring replacement of the furnace—$1200 or more.)	[ ]	[ ]
2. Do you smell gas around the furnace? (A very bad sign—call the gas company immediately.)	[ ]	[ ]
3. If there is radiant heating or heating that requires plumbing, are there any leaks?	[ ]	[ ]

Fireplace

Most people figure that there's little to go wrong with a fireplace. Unfortunately, that's not the case. The bricks in a fireplace can crack and the fireplace itself can pull away from the house (something which happens in earthquake country). This can lead to a dangerous situation in which the house can catch fire if the fireplace is used.

	YES	NO
1. From the outside, is there a separation between the fireplace and the house? (A separation is a big danger sign—have a professional check it out.)	[ ]	[ ]
2. Are there any visible cracks in the external bricks of the fireplace?	[ ]	[ ]
3. Are there any cracks in the firebricks inside the fireplace?	[ ]	[ ]

Tile

	YES	NO
1. Are there any cracks in the tile of the kitchen or bathrooms? (Cracks can simply be caused by dropping something heavy on the tile, or they can be symptomatic of house movements and a cracked foundation.)	[ ]	[ ]
2. Are floor tiles cracked? (Replacing cracked floor tiles when there is a problem with the floor simply means that the new tiles will soon crack. Fixing the floor problem could be very expensive.)	[ ]	[ ]

Termite Report

When you get a new loan, the lender almost always requires a termite clearance. This is a report from a registered termite company which states that the house is free of infestation.

It's important to understand that the report is of limited value. In areas where termites are endemic, there will always be some infestation. (The report usually states the house to be clear of termites for 60 days—the inspectors know that after that the termites will be back.)

In order to get a clearance, repair work must often be done. In some cases this is minor, involving the replacement of some wood and occasionally spraying. In other cases it is major, requiring the tenting of the house. Modern techniques may involve freezing the termites out of localized areas.

In most cases the termites chomp away at the wood structure of the home and are of little consequence. The real problem is that over 30 or 40 years, they can eat enough of the wood to make the house collapse.

	YES	NO
1. Is there a termite report?	[ ]	[ ]
2. Are you getting a termite clearance?	[ ]	[ ]
3. Will the seller pay for all repair work? (Normally the buyer pays for any preventive work.)	[ ]	[ ]

Hazards

Thus far we've been dealing with run-of-the-mill problems that you can look for in any home. There are, however, additional problems which may be of a hazardous nature. You should be aware of these and have a professional check for them.

Also, certain parts of the country are now requiring buyer and seller to sign off on some of these problems as well as other potential hazards. Be sure to check with your real estate agent about any conditions on the sale that the city, country, or state may impose.

	YES	NO
1. Asbestos ceilings?	[ ]	[ ]

Prior to about 1980, blown-in ceilings contained asbestos, which would then float down in invisible fibers. These ceilings may have to be scraped and removed or covered over with a sealant and a nonasbestos mixture. The cost for this is high.

	YES	NO
2. Wrapped asbestos pipes?	[ ]	[ ]

In some parts of the country, heating pipes under the house or in the basement were wrapped in asbestos insulation. This needs to be removed by experts and the pipes need to be rewrapped.

	YES	NO
3. Leaded copper pipe joints?	[ ]	[ ]

Prior to about 1986, the solder used to connect copper pipes in houses was made of a mixture of tin and lead. It was discovered that the lead would leach into water that sat in the pipes. Modern solders use a nonlead mixture. There is little that can be done about this short of resoldering all the copper joints. After about 5 years the leaching process tends to become minimal. It's mostly a problem in houses that are less than 5 years old. (You can run the water a while before using it to reduce the risk of lead poisoning.)

	YES	NO
4. Smoke alarms?	[ ]	[ ]

These should be installed on all floors and near kitchens and fireplaces.

	YES	NO
5. Insulation?	[ ]	[ ]

This isn't really a hazard. However, if you're in cold country without adequate insulation, you can be mighty uncomfortable. In an older house, the roof insulation usually can easily be brought up to modern building requirements. For walls, in some areas, holes were cut and a formaldehyde-based insulation shot in. The formaldehyde itself is a health hazard and where this has been done, sometimes the walls must be cut open and the insulation removed.

	YES	NO
6. Earthquake retrofitting?	[ ]	[ ]

In some parts of the country, particularly the West Coast, new laws are being proposed and are coming on line which require sellers to retrofit older homes and bring them up to earthquake safety standards. This may be something as simple as tying the framing down to the foundation or as complex as putting steel reinforcements from the foundation up to the roof. Be sure to check out what's necessary in your area and have the seller do the expensive work.

	YES	NO
7. Flood plain?	[ ]	[ ]

Some homes have been built on a flood plain. It may not flood more than once every 50 or 100 years. But if you own during that year, you lose. Often insurance is hard to get and expensive. Check it out.

	YES	NO
8. Radon gas hazard?	[ ]	[ ]

Radon is a naturally occurring gas in many soils. In some areas it can leak out of the ground and accumulate in the basement, and sometimes in other areas, of a house. It is a health hazard.

This is something which should be checked, particularly if you are in an area where radon gas leakage is common. Simple testing kits are available for under $50.

If radon gas does occur, an environmental engineer should be contacted to determine how it can be eliminated from the home. Often increasing the ventilation in a basement will do the trick. Other times expensive electronic venting systems are needed. In a few cases, it may be impossible to eliminate the hazard, in which case you may want to look elsewhere.

	YES	NO
9. Lead paint hazard?	[ ]	[ ]

If the house you are considering was built before the late 1970s (when lead paint was banned), chances are lead paint was used both inside and out. Lead is a serious health threat. It can produce sickness, retardation, and in extreme cases, even death. The most common means of getting lead poisoning is when children chew on molding or other painted areas of a house and ingest the lead paint. Sometimes old exterior paint containing lead will flake or dust off and contaminate the ground around the outside of the house where children play, and they may ingest some of the soil. The seller must present you with a disclosure statement regarding this hazard.

Safely removing lead paint is difficult and requires a qualified specialist. It can easily cost $10,000 or more to remove it properly from a home. On the other hand, many people simply paint over the lead paint with a nontoxic modern paint and hope for the best.

Few sellers are willing to pop for the cost of removing lead paint. Thus the choice becomes yours—are you willing to live in a house with this hazard? Many buyers of older homes who are made aware of the lead paint problem through the disclosure statement do move forward with the deal, but vow to watch their children more closely. If this problem bothers you, opt for a newer home.

14
Buying a Lot and Building Your Own Home

It's the dream of many couples to buy a lot, design, and then build their own home. It might be a vacation home in the woods. Or it might be in a suburban location. The common theme, however, is doing it yourself. Somehow, we all think, if we can just get the chance to build, we'll do it better than anyone else.

I know it was the dream of my wife and myself and we did do it in the north woods of Northern California a few years ago. The lessons we learned, as well as those of other self-builders with whom I've talked, can be extremely helpful if you're just starting on this course.

TIP

You can do it. It doesn't take as much money as you think. It doesn't take as much specialized knowledge. What it takes mostly is time and determination.

TRAP

Chances are you can't do it better than builders whose profession is putting up homes. They know materials and labor, design and construction, as well as where to cut corners and where to be lavish. But what you can offer that they can't is your own unique approach.

All of us should build our own home, once. It's an experience you'll cherish and never forget. And the home you produce will always have a warm spot in your heart.

How Do I Find a Lot?

The first thing you must do is find a lot. These days most people who construct their own home do it in rural or vacation areas (developers having already built up most suburban areas). Lots are for sale everywhere, but good lots are hard to find. Here's a check list of what to look for in a good lot:

Good Lot Checklist

Location

Everyone knows that location is important in real estate, but it is doubly important in rural or vacation areas. The reason is simple. Properties here take much longer to sell (frequently years). If you want to resell, you're going to need a prime location so you can get out relatively quickly. Does your lot have the following (in order of importance)?

	YES	NO
1. Waterfront (river or lake)?	[ ]	[ ]
2. View?	[ ]	[ ]
3. Level building site?	[ ]	[ ]
4. Easy access roads?	[ ]	[ ]
5. Close to urban/suburban area?	[ ]	[ ]

Lot Amenities

These are the features of the particular lot that you find. Some lots are grand while others are not so grand. Does yours have:

	YES	NO
1. Lots of trees?	[ ]	[ ]
2. A lot of room? (A minus in the city, but a plus in the country.)	[ ]	[ ]
3. Good soil? (It's harder to build in "rock country.")	[ ]	[ ]
4. A lot of level ground? (It's also harder to build on a mountainside.)	[ ]	[ ]

Water

In the city it's something you take for granted, but building in the country, it's a prime consideration. Does your lot have:

	YES	NO
1. A well? (Not so good)	[ ]	[ ]
2. A mutual or private water company (Good)	[ ]	[ ]
3. Water for irrigation? (Gardening)	[ ]	[ ]

Sewerage

It's something important to consider before you buy. Does your lot:

	YES	NO
1. Have access to a public a sewer system? (How much will it cost you to hook up to it?)	[ ]	[ ]
2. Require a septic tank? (Do you have enough room for a leach field?)	[ ]	[ ]

Power

Yes, many rural or mountain lots have not yet been accessed by the power company. It's a very big negative.

	YES	NO
1. Does your lot have electric power?	[ ]	[ ]
2. If not, is it coming soon?	[ ]	[ ]

Drainage

This can be a big factor later on, although it's something few of us remember to consider when we buy.

	YES	NO
1. Does your lot drain adequately?	[ ]	[ ]
2. Are there soft, wet areas indicating heavy water buildup?	[ ]	[ ]

	YES	NO
3. Will you need to dig drainage ditches before you build?	[ ]	[ ]

Title

Buying a lot is not quite the same as buying a house. You have to worry about all kinds of restrictions.

	YES	NO
1. Can you get clear title?	[ ]	[ ]
2. Are there any easements (to power companies, water companies, and so on) on your lot?	[ ]	[ ]
3. Are those easements just where you want to build? (If they are, you won't be able to.)	[ ]	[ ]
4. Are you in any kind of restricted area that would impair your ability to build:		
a. a coastal preserve?	[ ]	[ ]
b. a national forest?	[ ]	[ ]
c. a wildlife preserve?	[ ]	[ ]
d. other?	[ ]	[ ]
5. Is there a building moratorium in your area?	[ ]	[ ]

Environmental Concerns

These are important issues which you usually have to dig out.

	YES	NO
1. Is your area facing any kind of environmental impact control?	[ ]	[ ]
2. Is there something occurring in the area which would severely affect the value of your property:		
a. draining a lake?	[ ]	[ ]
b. changing the course of a river?	[ ]	[ ]
c. lumbering activity?	[ ]	[ ]
3. Is your lot located in a geologically unstable area (earthquakes)?	[ ]	[ ]

TIP

"Leach fields" are something new to many first-time home builders in rural areas. If you have a septic system, it is composed of two elements: the tank, which holds the solid sewerage, and the leach field, which drains out the liquid sewerage. A tank takes up only a few dozen square feet. A leach field, on the other hand, requires hundreds of square feet, usually in a flat area. Be sure you have enough room for your leach field as well as your building site when looking at a rural lot.

TRAP

Beware of lots that have their own wells. Chances are you'll be required to put in a septic tank for sewerage. Unless the lot is very large, the septic leach field may interfere with the well water. In short, it may be difficult to secure a building permit, and even if you do you stand the chance of poisoning yourself.

Also, many buyers look at their future lot in only one season. In the fall, for example, the lot may be dry and covered with beautiful foliage. However, in the spring, it may be a swamp from stagnant winter rain runoff.

Be sure to talk to local residents to get a picture of what your lot is going to be like all year long. Also look for ditches that neighbors have dug as well as natural water runoffs—these indicate the drainage of the lot. Beware of flat areas with no runoff, as they could become pools of water (or ice) in other seasons.

Finally, the quality of soil is a critical factor when building. Ideally, you want soil that allows water to percolate yet retains its shape. Expansive soils (mostly clays) expand when they get wet and this can easily lead to cracked foundations. Sandy soils can more easily wash away. If there is any doubt at all, get a soils report from a qualified engineering company.

Can I Finance the Lot?

Generally lots are paid for either in cash or with a mortgage carried back by the seller (typically for a term of under 10 years at prevailing interest rates). It would be a mistake to buy a lot thinking you can refinance it through a bank or savings and loan. S&Ls generally won't loan on bare land. Banks, when they will loan, generally will give only 50 percent or less of the appraised value.

TIP

Don't be hesitant to make a bold offer on financing a lot. For example, you may offer 10 percent down with the owners to carry a mortgage for the balance at 15 years at 2 percent below the current interest rate. Remember that lots are hard to sell and that frequently the people who own them, own them free and clear. You're not going to get such a favorable (to you) offer accepted every time, but you will get it accepted more often than you think.

Where Do I Get Building Plans?

Once you have your lot, the next step is to get a set of construction plans. This can be a very expensive or a very inexpensive task. At one end are the ready-made plans which are available through the mail from building magazines (just check your newsstands). At the other end of the spectrum you can hire an architect to draw up a set of plans just for you.

Mail-Order Plans

Mail order is definitely the cheapest way to go, since a set of plans can be obtained for just a few hundred dollars. There are literally thousands of mail-order plans available. Be sure you check to see that they are appropriate for your area of the country and that the building materials list doesn't involve some overly expensive timbers or metal.

TRAP

Be careful if you buy through-the-mail plans. A "working set" includes all elevations as well as details of all unusual construction. Some of the plans which I have seen sent through the mail are simply a front view and an inside view. They definitely give you enough to see what the house will look like, but they're a far cry from being detailed enough for you or a builder to work with. If you order through the mail, be sure that there is a full "money back" guarantee. In addition, as soon as you get the plans, take them to a builder to see if they are adequate.

TIP

Even if you order plans through the mail, you will probably have to modify them to accommodate your building site. Why not hire a local architect on an hourly basis to modify these plans? The cost can be a fraction of what drawing up a set of plans from scratch would be.

Custom-Made Plans

Custom-made is the most expensive way to go, but you can arrive at a unique and well-built house. You hire an architect to draft a set of plans for you. Typically, the cost is 3 to 5 percent of the cost of building the house. (If it costs $100,000 to build the house, figure $3000 to $5000 for the plans.)

A good architect will visit the building site and design the plans to fit the contour of the land. In addition, the architect will listen carefully to your desires for a home and incorporate those features that you want.

Finally, a good architect will be aware of building codes and of building materials costs in your area and will design a house to take advantage of whatever cost savings are possible.

TIP

Interview the architect as you would any other person you are hiring. Ask to see plans that the architect has previously done. (Sometimes you can save money by modifying an existing set of plans.) Find out who the architect has designed houses for and then call up those owners. Did they like the work? Did the architect take advantage of cost savings wherever possible? Would the owners recommend the person?

TRAP

Find out first what the costs will be. Some architects work on an hourly basis; others have a set fee. Don't assume that the costs will be minimal. Plans can be very expensive.

Do-It-Yourself Plans

In most areas of the country if you agree to live on the property for at least a year, you are permitted not only to do all the construction yourself but also to draw up the plans. No, this is not an impossible task. I've done it myself and I have no background in architecture or drafting.

What I did was to study the lot and then design a house that took advantage of the view. I then hired a draftsperson to create a set of working construction plans on the basis of my rough sketches. Finally I hired an engineer to determine the required loads. The total cost to me was under $1000. You can do it, too.

TIP

Work with your local building department, not against it. Find out in advance what special requirements it has (snow load, wind resistance, insulation, sewer systems, and so on). Incorporate these features into your plans at an early stage.

Get to know your local building inspectors and ask for advice. They may save you hours of time and thousands of dollars by suggesting approved methods of building that you may not have thought of.

How Do I Find a Good Builder?

Of course, you can build it all yourself, if you happen to be a relative of Hercules. However, some of the work is extremely hard, such as pouring concrete and lifting heavy timbers. Some requires special skills, such as soldering, plumbing, and plastering. And some is just plain tedious, such as putting up siding and sheet rock.

The alternative is to hire workpeople and/or a builder. Unless you plan to do at least 75 percent of the work yourself, you're better off striking a deal with a builder.

TRAP

Many builders are interested only in making a set profit on each job. When you submit a set of plans to them for a bid, they simply add up the square footage, multiply by a predetermined price, and that's your cost.

If you plan to do some of the work—finish the house, for example—you need to find a builder who actually does true cost estimates. These include finding out what the materials and labor will actually cost and then calculating profit on top of that. In the house I built, two builders went the first route, the third builder the other course. The third builder's price was 30 percent lower than that of the first two!

TIP

If you do most of the work yourself, you can hire workpeople to do the remaining chores for you. You can do, essentially, what the builder does. You can hire carpenters, plumbers, roofers, tapers, and so forth.

However, those you hire typically work on a "per job" basis instead of an hourly basis. They will want to see your plans and then will "bid the job." If they see you're inexperienced, they may give you a high bid. To avoid this, be sure that you get at least three bids for each job.

Checking Out Your Builder's Credentials

1. How many years has your builder been in the business in the area of your lot? (Three is usually considered a minimum.)?	________	
	YES	NO
2. Is your builder state-licensed?	[ ]	[ ]

	YES	NO
3. Have you called the state licensing bureau to see if there are any complaints against your builder?	[ ]	[ ]
4. Have you called the local better business bureau or district attorney's office to see if there are complaints?	[ ]	[ ]
5. Have you visited other houses your builder has constructed?	[ ]	[ ]
6. Did the prior construction look solid?	[ ]	[ ]
7. Did the owners voice any complaints?	[ ]	[ ]
8. Did you call the local building supply company to ask if your builder was ever late making payments?	[ ]	[ ]
9. Is your builder ready and able to get started?	[ ]	[ ]
10. Do you get along well with your builder?	[ ]	[ ]

TRAP

Most builders will want you to sign a building agreement in which you agree to provide them a series of payments out of which they will pay their workers and their materials suppliers. However, if you pay the builder and the builder does not pay the workers and suppliers, you could still be liable for full payment to those workers and suppliers. (They could file mechanic's liens on your property and force payment, even if you have to pay twice!)

Your only recourse, in such an event, may be to sue the builder, who may have filed for bankruptcy.

TIP

You can protect yourself by asking your builder to supply you with a completion bond. Most builders balk at this, however, because such bonds tend to be expensive and difficult to qualify for.

If you are securing financing in order to build, generally the lender will check out the builder and will withhold payments until the builder supplies proof of payment for labor and supplies. You can demand this proof (in the form of mechanic's "releases") too. Again, however, it's a hassle for the builder and many don't like doing it. In addition, sometimes the mechanics will give releases and then still file liens later on saying that the release was given on the builder's check and the lien was filed when that check bounced!

The greatest protection you can get is to insist on paying subcontractors and materials suppliers yourself. The builder submits a "chit" or authorization and you issue the check.

Again, however, builder's don't like doing this because it allows you to see exactly how much they are paying for labor and materials and how much profit they are making on your house.

The Construction Itself

Finally, you've bought the lot, had the plans drawn up, secured a builder (or hired subcontractors), and are ready to go. Once construction starts, plan on being there a great deal of the time or on having a builder or someone knowledgeable there to handle things.

There are always questions that pop up. What does that little squiggle on the plans mean? The plans call for a 3-foot foundation, but there's a 7-foot hole in the building site—what do we do? Where do you want the electrical switches? And on and on. Somebody has to be there to handle the questions.

TRAP

Don't count on the local building inspector to ensure that everything is done right. Building inspectors are notoriously lax. If you don't know how it should be built, hire someone who does to supervise the job.

TIP

Plan on spending more time than you first estimate. Workers don't show up on time. Building materials are delayed getting to the site. The weather turns against you. To be perfectly safe, use a rule of two. It takes twice as long to do anything as you think it will.

Buying a lot and building your own house is a wonderful experience. But as anyone who has done it will tell you, it's the sort of thing you only want to do once!

15
Is a Condo or Co-Op a Good Alternative?

The old adage was "Those who can, buy houses. Those who can't, buy condos and co-ops."

Times do change, however. Today, condos and co-ops are considered the first choice by many buyers instead of an unappealing second. Many people are even buying them as second homes in recreational areas. (Vacation property is no longer the exclusive realm of the rich, but is instead becoming increasingly important and available to many middle-income families.)

Thus you might be making just the right move when buying a condo or a co-op. Or maybe not. Let's see.

What Is a Condo?

A condominium, as most buyers know, involves a kind of shared ownership. Typically, you end up separately owning the inside of the unit while sharing with the other owners all the grounds, walkways, and recreational facilities—in short, everything outside. Another way to look at it is as if you were renting an apartment and then decided to buy your rental unit. (Indeed, some condos are converted apartment houses.)

It's sometimes useful to know that there are actually at least two separate kinds of condominium ownership. The first is the one with which most people are familiar—you could be on the fifth floor of a building and you own only that airspace that your unit occupies.

The second is sometimes called a townhouse (technically known as a PUD, or planned unit development). Here units are not arranged on top of one another. Rather, each unit has its own ground space below and airspace above. You actually own the ground beneath your townhouse.

What Is a Co-Op?

A co-op is a cooperatively owned property. This is a different sort of ownership in that you, as an individual, don't actually own any separate airspace or ground. Rather, you own a share of stock in a company which owns the entire property. While you have the exclusive right to use a particular unit, you don't actually own it in the sense of being able to sell it directly. To sell your unit, you must sell your share in the company.

What Are the Pros and Cons of Condo/Co-Op Living?

When you buy into a shared ownership property (either condo or co-op), you are actually trading off a portion of your privacy in exchange for reduced price (usually), guaranteed maintenance, and shared lifestyle. Condominium ownership is very much like living in an apartment. Your neighbors are only a thin wall away.

On the other hand, you usually (though not always) pay significantly less for condos and co-ops. Typically their prices are cheaper than single-family houses. In addition, since all the areas outside your unit are commonly owned, it is normally the responsibility of a homeowner association (HOA) to see to their care and grooming. Finally, often there are recreational amenities such as a swimming pool, rec room, tennis courts, and occasional parties that go along with condominium living.

TRAP

Regardless of what condominium promoters say, the fact is that during boom periods condos and co-ops are typically the last to see price appreciation, and during slumps they are the first to see price drops (except for urban shared properties, as noted below). This is primarily due to the perception of most Americans that condos and co-ops, while not quite second-class living, are still not as good as owning your own single-family home. (I'm not saying that I agree with this perception—only that it's an important factor in the marketplace.)

Therefore, don't be fooled into buying a condominium because it's cheaper than a similarly sized and located single-family home. Yes, it may be cheaper to buy, but chances are it will not appreciate as fast as a house and you'll have more trouble finding a buyer when it comes time to sell.

TIP

On the other hand, shared properties offer an opportunity to those who can't afford to buy a well-located single-family house. What you quickly learn when you first go house-hunting is that it's a very expensive proposition and often that first house is the hardest to afford.

A shared property can provide a marvelous first house. The price is often reasonable, the financing is roughly the same as for a single-family house, and you can get into a good location. Many first-time buyers purchase a condo or co-op and then live in it a few years, building up their equities. When they sell, they have a small nest egg that they can then apply toward a house.

What About Urban Condos and Co-Ops?

Thus far, we've been speaking primarily of shared properties which are located in the suburbs. However, in extremely high-priced urban areas, such as Manhattan, virtually no well-located single-family residences may be available at prices most people can afford. When that's the case, then shared living (most are co-ops there) has a different appeal.

TIP

Well-located urban shared properties have seen some of the highs and lows of the real estate market in general. Such units in Manhattan, Boston, and Washington, as well as parts of Chicago and Los Angeles, went up in price faster, on the whole, than single-family units in surrounding areas during the late 1980s. They also came down faster in the early 1990s.

It should be noted that in urban areas, particularly on the East Coast, the co-op has been the more popular vehicle of ownership. It has added a feature of exclusivity to the attractiveness of communal living. In a co-op, it may be the case that you cannot buy a share of the property unless and until the current owners vote you in.

While this has resulted in some excesses, many of which have been addressed by federal fair-housing legislation, what it has done is create the impression of a private club. Some co-op owners are able to charge much more for their ownership because of this perceived exclusivity.

Are There Any Special Problems with Shared Living?

There are some problems that go along with condo and co-op ownership. Besides the loss of privacy, these include the fact that you aren't "lord of all you survey." You normally can't paint the outside of your building or change the flower arrangement in front of your door if it is part of the common area. Even if you want to alter the interior of your unit (with the exception of simply changing the paint), you may have to get approval from the homeowner association.

TIP

Expect to spend some time on the homeowner association (or board of directors) if you buy into a shared property. If you don't, you'll find that the HOA is always doing something that you consider ridiculous and that you don't like. If you're a member, you'll want to be a part of decisions that affect your home and its value.

TRAP

Beware of HOA burnout. This comes after you've been a member of the board for a year or two and found that you can't get done what you want to get done. Often, owners will get discouraged and will sell their unit. If you're at least aware of this possibility, you may be less inclined to make such a drastic move when a stalemate does occur.

TIP

Look for a development with a low ratio of tenants to owners. The more rental units, the less desirable the place is for owners.

TRAP

Watch out for lawsuits against the HOA. They could restrict your ability to finance or sell your condo/co-op.

16
Should You Buy a New Home from a Builder?

In an average good year there are over 1 million new residential units built in the United States, most of them single-family residences or condos (as opposed to apartment buildings). While this is only perhaps a third or a fourth of the number of total home sales (the vast majority being resales of existing homes), it still represents a huge number of people. Perhaps you are considering the purchase of a new home instead of a resale. Are there different things to watch for? Are there special benefits as well as pitfalls to avoid?

The answers are all yes. While there are similarities, buying a new home is substantially different from buying a resale. It is a different market that requires you to have specialized knowledge.

Will a New Home or a Resale Appreciate Faster?

A question frequently asked by buyers is: "Where will I get the greatest appreciation—in a new home or in a resale?" (Or in a bad market, which home will go down in value least?) To put it another way: "If I had a choice between two houses, a brand new one and a resale each worth $100,000 and both in similar neighborhoods, which house would make me the most money or cost me the least money over the next 5 years?"

In the distant past the answer was generally the resale. The existing house had developed neighborhoods, schools, shopping, gardens, and so on. It had all the amenities already in place, and for that reason resales tended to appreciate more than new homes and to cost more as well.

During the 1980s, however, the tables turned. Then, in many areas of the country (but not all), the price appreciation on new homes was far and away greater than on resales. In addition, for the same number of square feet, new homes began to cost more than resales. (That only stands to reason—with inflation it costs more to build the same house today than it did 5 or 10 years ago.)

With the depressed real estate market of the early 1990s, buyers discovered that it didn't matter if a house was new or old, it could go down in value. Only those homes in the very best neighborhoods, new or old, kept their value or appreciated.

Today, if it were me, I would simply shop neighborhood first. (The fact is that no two neighborhoods are *exactly* alike.) This tends to favor resales, because their neighborhoods are established. However, many newer homes are being built in already established developments that are highly successful. I would avoid a new home in a new development in a new area.

TIP

Real estate is a localized market. That means that you cannot say that something is true at any given time for all parts of the country. While Southern California, for example, or the Northeast may see property values decline, at the same time parts of the Midwest may see them increase. That happened in the early 1990s.

TRAP

With regard to new homes, in general, in a hot market, the new houses will indeed appreciate faster than existing houses as noted above. However, in a stagnant and particularly in a declining market, new homes may not even hold their sales prices and large numbers of unpurchased, vacant homes (sometimes vandalized) can ruin the reputation of a new tract.

How Do I Find the Right New Home?

If you're determined to buy a new home, be prepared to spend some time looking. In most areas of the country, the era of the huge tract has given way to a few "spec" houses built here and there by builders. To see them all, you have to spend time traveling.

Many areas have a "buyer's guide" to new homes—a small magazine detailing the houses and their price range and showing maps of how to get there. The Sunday real estate section of any major newspaper almost always has ads for new homes.

What Should I Look for in a New Home?

Here's a checklist of items to look for when choosing a brand-new home.

New Home Checklist

1. *Number of bedrooms.* Three is ideal for resale, two may restrict your ability to resell quickly, four could make the house overbuilt for the area. __________?
2. *Number of bathrooms.* Two is minimal, three is better, four is overkill. __________?
3. *Ceilings.* High ceilings are in vogue. A better house will have at least one room with vaulted ceilings, usually a living or family room. __________?
4. *Kitchen.* Large and well-equipped kitchens sell houses. If your kitchen has an island in it complete with a stove, all the better. Is the oven self-cleaning? __________?
5. *Garage.* A two-car garage is a must. Three-car is better. ________?
6. *Additional rooms.* These are a plus, if they don't force the price out of sight. They include library, nursery, computer room, even a sound studio. __________?

7. *Yard.* Small yards are the rule today, given the high cost of land. Many families prefer small yards to avoid having to do extensive yard work. Large yards are considered luxury items and are found in more expensive homes. __________?
8. *Central air conditioning.* More and more it is considered to be a necessity, rather than a luxury. __________?
9. *High-quality insulation.* Check with the builder. The "R" rating should be the minimum required for the weather in your area. Higher "R" ratings will decrease your heating and cooling costs. Ask if the house was "wrapped" with a vapor/moisture barrier. It helps the insulation do its work. __________?
10. *Glass.* Are the sliding glass doors, bathroom windows, and other windows easily accessed by children made of "safety glass"? __________? Are they double-pane? __________?
11. *Electrical outlets.* The standard in most construction is one outlet every 12 feet of linear wall space. Extra outlets in kitchens and baths are a plus. __________?
12. *Floor coverings.* Wall-to-wall carpet is the rule in most new homes. Tiles are a plus. Hardwood floors are an additional plus, but remember, you'll have to buy carpet to put over them. __________?

How Do I Check Out a Neighborhood?

Here's a checklist to help you evaluate a neighborhood for a new home.

New Home Neighborhood Checklist

	YES	NO
1. Are the local schools good?	[ ]	[ ]
2. Are the schools nearby?	[ ]	[ ]
3. Are there day-care facilities nearby?	[ ]	[ ]
4. Is the area relatively crime free?	[ ]	[ ]
5. Is the police department responsive?	[ ]	[ ]
6. Is there adequate fire protection?	[ ]	[ ]

	YES	NO
7. Is shopping nearby?	[ ]	[ ]
8. Is there a hospital nearby?	[ ]	[ ]
9. Is the neighborhood "quiet"?	[ ]	[ ]
10. Are posted speed limits slow?	[ ]	[ ]
11. Is there a high-traffic street nearby?	[ ]	[ ]
12. Is there a park nearby?	[ ]	[ ]
13. Is public transportation available?	[ ]	[ ]
14. Is there adequate off-street parking?	[ ]	[ ]
15. Are the lots "private" enough?	[ ]	[ ]
16. Is the tract landscaped?	[ ]	[ ]
17. Is there danger of future erosion?	[ ]	[ ]
18. Does the water system provide pure drinking water?	[ ]	[ ]
19. Are there any special assessments that you'll have to pay (street improvement, sewer tax, and so on)?	[ ]	[ ]
20. Are there any nearby hazards or nuisances (factories, swamps or rivers, oil tanks, hazardous waste facilities, and so on)?	[ ]	[ ]
21. Are you connected to a sewer system (septic systems are less desirable)?	[ ]	[ ]

In addition to the features of the house itself as well as the neighborhood, there is the factor of the marketplace. The housing market is volatile, with many ups and downs. Here's what to look for in a variety of different markets.

How Do I Judge the New-House Market?

In a stable market (no rapid price appreciation or depreciation), there are more new homes than buyers, and builders are anxious to sell them off. The ads for the homes are placed in all papers, there are signs along the major roads directing you to the new tracts, and there are almost always models of all the homes available to see.

While the salespeople in the office try to get you to make a quick decision, remember that you usually have plenty of time. You can leisurely shop around, going from model to model until you find just the right home for you. Once you find it, you can often negotiate more favorable terms from the builder (reduced price, a buydown on the loan—where the builder pays part of your interest for a few years—free amenities such as fences, yards, and so forth). This is the ideal market in which to buy a new home. In a sense, it's a "buyer's market" and you're sitting in the driver's seat.

TIP

Try to find the medium-size home in the best-located tract—this property will appreciate the fastest. (The smallest home may be simply too small for many buyers and could be a white elephant; the largest home is often too expensive when it comes time for resale.)

What If the Market Is Depressed?

You'll know a depressed market if you're in it. Every Sunday the paper will offer "repos" and "REOs" and "bank-owned properties" for sale or auction. It's been the rule rather than the exception in many parts of the country for several years.

If the ads don't alert you, there are other signs of a down market:

- Statistics available from brokers and published in the business section of the local papers indicate that the volume of home sales is off from last year.
- The number of houses advertised for sale (both new and resale) in the newspapers is enormous.
- The price of homes is declining. This is usually measured by the median price. Instead of going up, statistics may suggest it's declining.
- Government home auctions by the FHA (Federal Housing Administration) or the VA (Veterans Administration) may be held weekly, as evidenced by large ads in local papers.
- There's difficulty getting financing from lenders because of the many houses already in default.
- Tracts of new homes are fully built with the houses standing vacant and unsold.

TIP

Be wary of buying a new home in this market. In a down market you can find "steals" on resales as desperate sellers fight to get out. On the other hand, builders are limited in how much they can drop their prices. They generally operate on thin margins, and the houses are financed for most of their value. Sometimes you can buy a home that the same builder sold a year ago from an original buyer for much less than you can buy the same model brand new from the builder today.

What About Buying a New Home When the Market's Hot?

A hot market may be the most difficult time to buy a home. Hot markets have occurred on both coasts at various times over the past 50 years, although not usually in the recent past. Generally the hot market doesn't last for more than 18 to 24 months. But during that time, it's like living in a different world.

What happens in a hot market is that there are more buyers than there are homes available for sale, both resales and new. (The reason is that prices are perceived to be going up, and speculators enter the market as well as people who buy with the intention of occupying the property.)

In a hot market, prices go up for both resales and new homes. However, they tend to go up faster for new homes. As a result, speculators enter the market attempting to lock in a price and then quickly resell at a much higher price.

When you are seeking a new home in a hot market, the odds are set against you. You are competing against other buyers for relatively few homes. Builders don't need to advertise, since buyers are beating the woods looking for new homes, so it's hard to locate the tracts. And frequently the prices of the new homes are so high that it's scary.

The Early Bird Gets the Worm

Here's a story that may seem totally out of place in a down market, but that is perfectly commonplace when the market heats up. I have a friend who wanted to buy a brand-new home in a suburb of San Francisco. This was at a time when the market was almost too hot to touch.

However, my friend was determined. Each day after work Jerry would cruise the neighborhood looking for signs of new construction—lots being bulldozed, houses being framed, even signs indicating that a builder was going to develop a tract on a certain piece of land.

Eventually Jerry located a tract he liked. It was the second phase of a builder's earlier development. When Jerry found it, the lots were just being bulldozed. No construction had started.

There really was no one there to talk to. So Jerry flagged down a bulldozer driver and asked where he could find the construction foreman. From that person he learned who the developer was and called the developer's office.

The developer told him that while she had plans for the houses being constructed, she hadn't yet finalized plans for their cost. She took his name and promised to call him back as soon as she had calculated how much the houses would sell for.

Jerry didn't take any chances. He called her every week for 2 months until finally she gave him a price list and indicated that the construction company would begin accepting offers to purchase on June 10, a month hence.

Jerry got a copy of the plans (the models weren't yet built) and went around to the building sites, deciding finally on a particular lot and design he preferred. The cost was $35,000 more than he thought he could afford (see Chapter 5 to determine what you can afford), however, he borrowed from his parents in order to be sure he could buy the house.

Four days before the builder was going to accept offers Jerry, complete with cot, sleeping bag, thermos, and ice chest filled with food, set up residence in front of the builder's office. Mind you, this was 4 days early.

Jerry was the first one there. However, within hours of his arrival, half a dozen other people showed up and camped out behind him. By the next day the line had swollen to over two dozen. Two days before the houses were to go on sale, there were over 50 people in line. Keep in mind, only 28 houses were going to be sold.

To help keep things orderly, Jerry made a list of who was in line in what position and gave it to the developer, who agreed to honor it.

Finally the fateful day arrived. Jerry was the first one in, the first to give his deposit, the first to sign a sales agreement. (There obviously was no haggling on price or terms—Jerry accepted whatever the builder dictated.) Then he went home to the first decent night's sleep in nearly a week.

It took 6 months to build the homes. Finally, after some harrowing troubles with qualifying for the lender (Jerry borrowed extra money from relatives), he got the house and moved in. His house came with no fences, no yard, and very few amenities inside. He paid more than he wanted to, but he was in.

Question: Was it a good move for Jerry?

Depends when you ask. Three months after Jerry moved in, he was offered a $55,000 profit if he would sell. He laughed and hung on. A year later the housing depression hit California. As of this writing his house is worth about $20,000 less than he paid.

TIP

In a hot market the builder/developer really doesn't need to bother with marginal buyers. Be sure that you have the necessary down payment lined up in advance and that you can qualify for the financing.

TRAP

Markets go both ways. Sometimes the most important thing is knowing when to take your profit.

Should You Buy a Built or Yet-to-Be-Built New Home?

In most stable markets you often have a choice between buying an already built home or one that a builder has yet to put up. There are pros and cons with going each way.

With the already built home, you know what you're getting and usually can see the neighborhood. But, with the yet-to-be-built home, items can be changed to fit your specific needs.

My suggestion is that whenever possible, always buy a home that is already built. I believe that knowing what you're going to get is more important than being able to customize a plan. Besides, you know for certain that it's actually going to get built.

Will You Really Get the New Home You Buy?

Another friend of mine wanted to buy a new home in a development in Orange County, south of Los Angeles. Jill loved the location and fell in love with one of the models. There were several homes already constructed and ready for sale, but not the model she wanted. (This was during a stable period in the area.) The builder told Jill that her model would be available in the "next phase." He took a $500 refundable deposit from her and signed an agreement, explaining that she would be required to fill out a sales agreement as soon as the house was built. The $500 merely reserved the house for her. He guessed that it would be ready in 3½ months.

Four months later the builder hadn't even broken ground. Jill, and a number of others, were haunting his offices trying to find out what the problem was. All she could get were vague answers. She was told that the lenders would not agree to the financing because of some title problems. Or there was a permit difficulty with the city. Or the builder was waiting until materials costs came down. Or something else.

Finally, 5½ months after Jill paid her deposit, work began. It took another 5½ months to finish her home.

During the building period, she visited the home whenever she could, sometimes several visits a week. She didn't notice any problems until the house was almost completed and the wallboards put up. Then she realized that the floor plan was not exactly the same as the model. The windows of the living room didn't face the hills, the one feature she admired most about the plan.

She confronted the builder (after he missed three appointments to see her). Yes, he explained, the plans were changed. Building costs had changed and he was just adjusting to them. A few corners had been cut here and there so that he could deliver the property at the agreed-upon price.

What could she do? She continued to wait.

Finally, the building was completed. It wasn't at all what Jill hoped it would be. But after all the waiting (nearly 10 months), she was glad she would be able to move in.

When she went to sign the sales agreement, however, she found that the price had gone up by $11,000!

How could that be, she wanted to know? She had agreed upon a price with the builder. He pointed out that the price he agreed upon was the price of 11 months earlier. Costs had gone up since then, not only the price of building materials and labor but also the interest rate he was paying on his construction loan. He pointed to a clause in their agreement which clearly stated he could adjust the price to reflect any increased costs.

In the end, it wasn't the house Jill wanted at the price she wanted to pay. She got her $500 deposit back and began to look elsewhere. However, she had lost nearly a year, not to mention all the hassle.

Yes, this is a true story. No, it doesn't happen all the time. It probably doesn't happen most of the time (although price and plan changes are legend in construction). But it does happen enough that you should be aware of it and at least plan on the possibility.

What's Extra When I Buy a New Home?

Have you noticed that when you buy a new car, you almost never get it for the base sticker price? Invariably, you end up paying more for extras. Buying a new home is not dissimilar.

When you buy a new home, there are lots of extras. These fall into two categories: extra items (such as fences) and upgrades to a better quality of item (such as carpets). Here's a list of some of the extras and upgrades you can expect to pay more for:

1. Larger or view lot
2. Any changes in the basic construction plan
3. Fences
4. Landscaped yard
5. Upgrade of roof
6. Upgrade of exterior walls
7. Upgrade of carpet or tile
8. Air conditioning (now standard on many homes)
9. Additional mirrors or windows
10. Upgrade of insulation
11. Upgrade of appliances (stove, oven, dishwasher, refrigerator)
12. Upgrade of plumbing fixtures (toilets, sinks, tubs)
13. Larger water heater

Many builders have a list of upgrades that they strictly adhere to. For example, you have your choice of three grades of carpet and that's it. Or you can choose from six tile patterns, three of which cost extra, no changes allowed.

There are several reasons that builders limit the changes and upgrades you can make. One is cost. They get guaranteed estimates from a few distributors and they know what it's going to cost to purchase a particular product. That makes it easy for them to stick with that product.

Also, there's the cost of labor as well as materials. Some materials require extra labor costs. For example, some Japanese tiles are irregular (when compared with American or European tiles), and there may be an extra labor charge for installing them. To avoid hassles here, the builder may simply limit the selection to half a dozen patterns, all because he knows he can control the labor costs.

Finally, there's the matter of lender and building department approval. The builder usually has lenders who have guaranteed approval of financing, provided the house is built a certain way with certain features. Change the features and a new appraisal might be necessary. Similarly, the plans may call for specific features. Change those features and the builder may have to submit new plans to the building department.

The real question you should ask yourself is: Which upgrades and extras are worthwhile and which are not? Here are some clues.

Larger or View Lot

The price isn't usually that much more. For example, a lot with a view may cost $5000 more than a lot without. A larger lot may cost $1500 more than a standard lot.

TIP

If you buy a view lot, it's the best money you can spend. You'll get it back times over when you sell.

TRAP

If you buy a larger lot, beware. Unless you landscape it so that it requires little to no maintenance work, it could be a drawback when you resell.

Fences

In those areas of the country where fences are common, you're going to need a fence. Expect to pay more for it perhaps half the time.

TIP

It's often simpler to let the builder put up a fence (particularly if there are architectural or building restrictions) at the time the house is constructed than to put it up yourself. However, that may not be the cheapest route. Often an independent fence contractor can beat the builder's price. Finally, if you're handy, you can beat both prices substantially by doing it yourself.

Carpets and Floor Coverings

Usually new homes come with wall-to-wall carpet, tile, and/or finished wood. But the quality of these often leaves much to be desired. The difference is most obvious with carpets and tiles. The model home may have luxurious, thick carpeting, whereas the actual carpeting that comes with the home may be short and threadbare. The model may have colorful Italian tiles while the standard home comes with ordinary white tiles.

TIP

It usually doesn't pay to upgrade to the most expensive tile or carpet. But it usually does pay to upgrade to a medium-quality, for two reasons. First, at least in terms of carpet, it ensures that the floor covering will last more than just a few years. Second, it helps ensure that the carpet will look good, a particularly important point if you want to resell in a few years. (Carpets make the biggest impression on potential home buyers: Don't you look at them first?) Besides, upgrading carpet from low grade to medium usually isn't that expensive.

TRAP

Be careful of upgrading tiles. The cost of tiles varies enormously. Some tiles may be only a dollar a square foot. Others may be $100 a square foot or more! Colorful tiles are nice, but for resale, clean, unbroken regular tiles will usually do just as well.

Yard

Some builders will put in yards, front and back, for you if you wish. Except for one case, explained shortly, this is usually an expensive trap. Putting in yards can be very costly. On the other hand, if you do some of the work yourself and hire out only the difficult tasks like installing the plumbing and planting large trees, you can do it for significantly less.

The one exception is the front yard in tracts which have architectural control. The CC&Rs (covenants, conditions, and restrictions) which govern the tract may require a certain type of front yard. Certain bushes, certain arrangements, certain watering patterns may be required.

Often, when architectural control of front yards is required, the cost is automatically included in the price of the house and the builder automatically puts in the yard. But not always. Sometimes you have the option of paying the builder or doing it yourself.

My advice is that in this case, let the builder do it. You will save hassles arguing with the architectural committee, sprained backs (as you try to put in a pineapple tree that weighs three times as much as you do), and possibly even money.

Air Conditioning

If air conditioning is offered as an option (instead of a standard feature), get it. The climate appears to be growing warmer in most parts of the country. Today, just as in automobiles, air conditioning is considered to be a necessary feature. You may find that you have trouble selling your house later on if it doesn't have air.

TRAP

Most other options and upgrades (roof, exterior walls, mirrors or windows, added insulation, appliances, larger water heater) are usually a waste of your money. You'll have trouble getting the investment back later on when you go to resell. (The exception is when the standard appliances that comes with the house are especially shoddy.)

How Should I Watch Out for Shoddy Construction?

One of the advantages of buying a resale is that you pretty well know what you're getting. If the home has been standing for 5, 10, or more years, chances are it will stand another 30 or 40.

On the other hand, when you purchase a new home, you're buying something that is as yet untried. If there are defects, they could show up in the first few years of usage.

But, I hear many readers saying, aren't new homes fully inspected by city or county building departments? Don't they have to meet strict health and safety guidelines?

Yes—and no. All modern buildings are inspected at numerous times during their construction. In most cases, the inspector catches problems and forces their correction before a "certificate of occupancy" is granted. (You can't occupy the home without this certificate—in most areas you can't even connect to water, power, or gas without it.)

However, there may be only one or two building inspectors and hundreds of houses to inspect. Further, while in most cases the inspectors are well trained and experienced, they often are not expert in every area of construction. And in a few cases they simply are not very well qualified.

The upshot of all this is the fact that regardless of the area of the country, shoddy construction goes on all the time right next to excellent construction. For example, a few years ago the builder of a housing tract in Southern California decided to use a Spanish tile roof. This consists of red, curved tiles interlaced to form a very attractive roof line.

The trouble with the tiles is that they aren't very good at holding out water. In a wind-driven storm, the water sweeps up under the edges of the tiles and through the roofs. In the old days (the 1700s) Spanish tile roofs were used extensively in California. However, in those days a kind of mortar was applied to the roof and the tiles were carefully set into it. This effectively waterproofed them.

Today the use of this mortar would be unattractive and expensive. So instead, roofers lay down layers of heavy, waterproof felt before placing the tiles. It acts as an effective water barrier.

However, in this particular tract the roofer had never before laid Spanish tiles. No felt was placed beneath them. The building inspector, also unfamiliar with the need for felt, didn't catch it.

You're right. With the first rain the roofs leaked—every roof in a tract of over 60 houses! About two-thirds had been sold and the water damage forced the occupants out. Needless to say, they were furious and everyone looked to the builder for repairs.

The builder was an honorable person, but not particularly wealthy. All the tiles on the roofs had to be removed and felt placed underneath. It meant reroofing over 60 homes—a very, very costly thing to do. The builder simply couldn't handle it and declared bankruptcy.

The homes that hadn't been sold were taken back by the lender, who corrected the problem. But the two-thirds that had been sold ended up being the responsibility of the owners. It cost about $10,000 per house for the repairs.

Note, this was shoddy construction. But no one was really trying to cut corners. It was just a case of a builder working in an area of unfamiliarity and a building inspector likewise being in the dark.

Unfortunately, this isn't an isolated case. In another tract of new homes in a neighboring state, the builder did not use approved metal fittings to join the heavy timbers that held the ceiling of the house to the beams that supported them. Again, for some inexplicable reason, the building inspector didn't catch it. As a result, a few years after the houses had all been sold out, they began shifting. Cracks appeared in the ceilings and walls, and in one case a dining room ceiling crashed down onto the dining room table (fortunately, there were no injuries).

Complaints from homeowners caused a thorough investigation by the city, which then condemned the houses and forbade anyone to live in them until the problems were corrected! The owners had to move out. The retrofitting of the metal braces required cutting into walls and ceilings and cost thousands of dollars per house. Again, the builder declared bankruptcy and the owners were left to their own resources to make the repairs.

Of course, these are exceptions. Most buyers of new homes have no problems at all (or small problems which the builder quickly fixes). But that doesn't mean that major structural problems in workmanship or even materials couldn't occur. In a way it's again like buying a car. Chances are the one you get will be wonderful. On the other hand, you could get a lemon.

What About Builder Warranties?

Nearly all builders back their construction with warranties. Even a builder who does not give you a written warranty may be offering you an "implied" warranty, depending upon the state in which you live. Today many states have strong consumer protection laws which allow you to take the builder to court for shoddy construction, and win a settlement. (Of course, that's of dubious value if the builder has gone broke.) Often the warranties run for 10 years or more.

Of that vast majority of builders who offer warranties, there are two groups: Those who self-warrant and those who buy insurance.

Self-Warranted Homes

A builder who self-warrants a home will normally give you a certificate of warranty, which states what is covered and what is not covered. Typically such a warranty says that if it's not specifically noted, it's not covered.

The Magnuson-Moss Act (1975) is a disclosure law which is handled by the Federal Trade Commission (FTC). Under Magnuson-Moss, a warranty issue by a builder must include the following:

1. The name of the person who is warranted (you) and a specific statement of whether the warranty is transferable if you sell the property.

2. Precise information on what is covered and what is excluded.
3. Exact language detailing what a builder will do to correct a problem that arises.
4. The length of the warranty.
5. The procedure, in detail, for filing a claim.
6. Any limitations on consequential damages. (Consequential damages result as a consequence of covered problems. The most common example is a water pipe bursting causing damage to furniture. The pipe may be covered, but is the furniture?)
7. A clear statement of any reduction of implied warranties.

TRAP

As part of the warranty, some builders have the buyers sign a statement that they waive all implied warranties. In the states that permit this, if you sign such a statement, you may give up more rights than you get, since the implied warranties may be stronger than the builder's specific warranties. If a builder insists you sign a waiver statement, you may want to consider a different builder and house.

Under a builder's warranty, you have to go back to the builder to get satisfaction if a problem arises. It's to your advantage, therefore, to find a builder who is big enough to sustain the losses involved with any problems. (Note the examples above.) We'll have more to say on selecting the right builder shortly.

Insurance-Warranted Homes

A different kind of warranty is offered by a large group of builders nationwide. This is a warranty backed not only by the builder but also by an insurance company. Typically under these policies the builder continues to warrant the house, but the insurance company backs up that warranty. In addition, it offers a plan that changes with the years the house is in existence, offering greater protection in the first years and less in the later ones.

TIP

Many insurance-backed warranties are transferable. However, there may be limitations and exclusions. Usually under these plans, your first recourse is to seek a solution to the problem from the builder. If the builder does not or is not able to comply, the insurance company picks up the tab for covered items after a deductible is paid.

How Do I Find a Good Builder?

Most of us simply shop houses. We go from tract to tract trying to find the new home that will be just right for us. It's also important, however, to shop builders. As should be evident from the discussions on shoddy workmanship and on warranties, a lot depends on the builder. You want a builder who does good work and who has the means to back it up should any unforeseen problems arise.

Here's a checklist to help determine the quality of the builder.

Checklist for Selecting a Builder

1. How long has the builder been constructing new homes? (Longevity is always a good sign.) __________?

	YES	NO
2. Can you get a recommendation (or a condemnation!) from a relative, friend, or associate who's previously had dealings with the builder?	[ ]	[ ]
3. Check with the Better Business Bureau. This organization normally keeps complaints filed against businesses. Does the builder have many complaints filed?	[ ]	[ ]

4. Check with any consumer groups active in the area. Also check with the local office of the National Association of Home Builders. Your builder should be a member of this group and it may be able to give a recommendation. __________
5. Find out where the builder has previously built new homes. Go to the tract and knock on a few doors.

Simply say you are going to be buying a home from the same builder and you would like to know if those who bought before had any difficulties, such as shoddy work or reluctance to fix problems. Don't be embarrassed. Homeowners love to talk about their builder. Either she's wonderful and has done a marvelous job. Or he's been a disaster for them. Just be sure you talk to more than one person to get a balanced viewpoint.

Can I Negotiate with the Builder?

Now we come to the tricky part for many new home buyers: negotiating with the builder. Here many who purchase a new home are completely lost, signing anything and everything that is placed before them.

TIP

Just as with purchasing a resale, when buying a new home everything is negotiable. The problem with new homes, however, is that the builder is often tied into financing and labor and materials contracts so that he or she cannot really offer the flexibility that an owner of a resale can.

Typically when buying a new home, you are presented with a colorful and expensive-looking brochure which gives the floor plans of the various models that the builder is offering. Along with these is usually a price schedule. For Plan A the price is $85,000 until January 2, when the price goes up to $87,500. For Plan B the price is $135,000. For Plan C it's $168,000. And so forth. In addition, there are higher costs for better lots as well as additional costs for upgrades, as described earlier.

Thus, the prices are laid out in the same fashion as they are in a grocery store. You certainly can't bargain with the grocer over the price of a jar of mayonnaise. How do you bargain with a builder over the price list for a new home?

TRAP

It's important to understand that builders and developers like to create the impression that nothing is negotiable—either you take their price or you don't get the house. That's part of the reason for the elaborate brochures. The truth, however, is that builders are sellers just like any other sellers. When builders need to get rid of homes, they will negotiate down to the bare bones, regardless of what the brochures say.

The way you negotiate with builders is to say that you would "like to submit an offer on one of the houses." The salesperson should be a licensed real estate agent and he or she, acting as a fiduciary for the builder, must submit all offers (unless the builder has stipulated in writing that no offers be submitted below a specific price—an unlikely possibility). The trick, of course, is to make the offer reasonable.

The easiest way to negotiate is to find a builder who already has houses up, to accept the price, and then bargain over the "extras." Yes, you'll pay the price, but you want complete fencing around the property, you want an upgrade of carpet at no additional cost to you, and you want a self-cleaning oven instead of the standard oven included with the home.

In a flat market with already constructed homes, as noted earlier in this chapter, the builder might very well consider such an offer. After all, the builder gets the fencing, the carpeting, and the stove at wholesale. Why not pay the additional charges to get rid of a home that's costing the builder upward of thousands of dollars a month in interest charges?

TIP

As noted earlier, don't expect the builder to budge when the market's hot or when the houses haven't yet been constructed. In this case, there's no leverage on your side. Why should the builder accept a lower offer when there are other buyers willing to pay full price or when the builder hasn't even put up the houses and isn't paying interest on them?

Don't Forget Terms

Another bargaining point is terms. This is often the case when interest rates are higher and it's difficult to qualify for mortgages. The builder may be willing to "pay down" the mortgage by several points. For example, you'll get the mortgage. However, instead of paying the going rate of, say, 9 percent for the first 3 years, you might pay 7 percent, with the builder paying the other 2 percent. On a $100,000 mortgage, 2 percentage points can save you roughly $2000 a year in interest payments.

TRAP

Beware of builders who pay down the mortgage, then raise the price by an offsetting amount. In the above example, you would save close to $6000 over a 3-year buydown. But if the builder raised the price of the property by $6000, where would be your savings? You'd be converting a lower payment into a higher price. And after the first 3 years, you'd be paying mortgage interest on that higher price.

In most cases, a builder won't buy down an interest rate unless the houses have been sitting around for a long time and the builder is anxious to get rid of them. If that's the case, by talking to those who bought 6 months ago in the same tract, you should be able to establish what the original pricing was. Thus, you can determine if the builder has raised the price to pay for your buydown.

Negotiating Price

Finally, you can negotiate price with a builder, although your chances of getting a significant reduction could be slim. Here's the reason.

Builders usually operate on a fairly tight margin: 10 to 25 percent profit. Let's consider a builder who is working with a 10 percent margin building homes that are priced to sell in the $100,000 range. The builder's profit is $10,000, meaning the house costs roughly $90,000 to construct (including land).

It's important to understand that the builder almost never puts up the entire $90,000 to build the home. Rather, he or she usually buys the land and then borrows the money under a construction loan from a lender to erect the building. Let's say in our example that the land costs 25 percent of the selling price, or $25,000. Thus the house actually costs $65,000 to build.

Building costs	$ 65,000
Land	$ 25,000
Profit	$ 10,000
Selling price	$100,000

The builder has a loan for $65,000 on the house, on which interest must be paid monthly. In addition, there are charges for taxes and insurance. Typically the interest charges as well as the costs for taxes and insurance during the building period and for perhaps a month or two afterward have been factored into the $65,000 cost of construction.

However, if the builder puts up the houses and they don't sell during the allotted period, then the costs for interest, taxes, and insurance begin to come out of her or his pocket. Thus after the construction period, the builder in this example might be paying out close to $1000 a month while waiting for a buyer.

It's easy to see that after a while, the builder would have used up all the profit. Thus, as time goes buy he or she becomes increasingly anxious to sell. Your chances of getting a better deal improve the longer the houses have been constructed and are sitting there.

On the other hand, the longer the houses are sitting there, the less the builder can lower the price. If the houses have been sitting for 10 months and the builder has paid out $5000 of the profit margin, there is only $5000 in profit left to make. If you offer $5000 less than the selling price, the builder will make no profit and is likely to turn you down. Perhaps a drop in price of $1000 or $2000 might be accepted. But the builder simply can't afford to take much less.

That's why it's not very likely that you'll be able to bargain a builder down in price. Better to go for extras, upgrades, or terms.

TIP

In a bad market, the builder may go bankrupt. If so, the bank takes over and may be forced to sell for much less in order to get rid of the properties. You'd get a better price.

Keep in mind that, as with cars, the higher the house is priced, the more bargaining room a builder may have. If you're in the $300,000 price range or higher, the profit may go up significantly. Thus, the higher the price, the more chance you have of negotiating a price reduction.

17
What About Buying a Vacation Home?

Vacation homes used to be the exclusive realm of the famous and the rich. But times change. Today, vacations homes are increasingly important as the second home of many middle-income families. More and more people buy and enjoy vacation homes. Will you?

A vacation home can be a cabin in the woods or a condo in another city. It can be big or small, fancy or plain. Spurred by the need to get away from the crowding of cities and lured by the thought of acquiring some potentially valuable land, many people have bought a vacation property. Almost always, however, it's a second home. Few of us have the time or resources to live year round at a vacation home.

Vacation homes are really quite different from other types of homes. However, they do share some of the problems. Here, we're going to concentrate on economic issues.

Vacation homes are expensive, very expensive. Assuming you finance the purchase, you will have an additional set of mortgage payments to make. Plus you'll have a second set of taxes and insurance to worry about. Then there are utilities, upkeep, homeowner's dues (if you're in a shared community setting), fire protection, and a host of other concerns.

Quite frankly, from a strictly economic perspective, a second home makes little financial sense.

TIP

Often you can rent out a second or vacation home. You may be able to recoup much of your costs by renting it out only part of the time. In recreational areas, often you can rent out a property weekly for a few months and make enough money to pay for its annual costs.

On the other hand, you may be able to write off a portion of your expenses and avoid paying a portion of your income. The tax law on write-offs is about to change as this chapter is written, so you'll want to consult your accountant for the details.

TRAP

If you rent out your vacation home, don't expect the tenants to take as good care of it as you would. This is particularly the case with rapid turnover—when you're renting on a weekly or monthly basis. You won't want to have good furniture in the place or anything you consider precious. All these considerations make many people regret the fact that they rent out their property.

Will I Have Trouble Reselling?

You could. Unlike suburban or urban homes, vacation property, particularly rural vacation property, is highly illiquid. (All real estate is illiquid, but vacation property more so.)

If you have a house in a city neighborhood, there's always going to be a buyer for it. In a bad market you may have to lower your price or offer seller financing. But if you make the property attractive enough, a buyer will come along and take it.

With vacation property, however, that's not the case. During boom periods, particularly when people are feeling good about the economy and want to find places to "get away" to, vacation property thrives. Buyers are almost knocking on your door.

On the other hand, during economic slumps when people are more concerned about keeping their jobs than taking a vacation, you find that there are no buyers at all. That's right. It may not matter how low you reduce your price or how favorable the terms—there may simply be no buyers available.

TIP

Consider the purchase of a vacation/second home only as a long-term proposition. Once you buy, figure you are going to be stuck with the property for a minimum of 3 to 5 years. Tell yourself that if you want to sell, it could take you that long to find a buyer! (That's not an exaggeration in many areas.)

Of course, you could have buyers lining up outside. But don't count on it. If you figure that the day you buy is the worst day of the worst month of the worst year for vacation property, you won't go far wrong—and you could end up doing quite well.

Vacation property—a second home—is a risky venture. As noted, in the past it was for the rich, who could afford it. Today, it's for everyone, including many of us who can't afford it.

Before you jump in, take a long, hard look at your financing, particularly several years down the road. Will you need the money you invest today in your vacation home for something else later on (such as the kids' education)? If so, will you be able to get it out?

On the other hand, we don't live by bread alone. Life in the city can be too competitive, too noisy, too crowded. Sometimes the only answer is a second or a vacation home.

18 When You Have a Problem

What do you do when you buy and things don't work out as you had hoped? What do you do when things go very badly?

You've paid your money, you have your mortgage, and escrow has closed. A set of keys has been delivered into your hands as well as hearty congratulations from all concerned. You're now the proud owner of a new home.

Now what?

Things will go wrong, count on it. It's simply inevitable. What's important is how you classify the problems and how you react to them. In this chapter we're going to try to separate the ordinary from the serious problem; we're going to look at what might go wrong and how to correct it—after the close.

TRAP

Most buyers feel that the problems with a purchase end with the end of escrow. Sometimes that's true, but in other cases your problems are only just beginning.

Don't Sweat the Small Stuff

The small stuff includes a screen door that doesn't quite close. Or a garbage disposer that works, but is noisy. Or burned-out bulbs in the ceiling fixtures. Or…you get the idea. These are minor annoyances. Don't call the seller or the agent. Just deal with them yourself.

Sometimes, however, you may actually be responsible for the problem. For example, you try to move in, but there's no heat, no water, and no light. What should you have done?

You have to get connected. If you overlook this, you'll have a problem after escrow because utilities and other services typically take up to a week or more to connect. Therefore, as soon as you're sure the deal is going to go through (before escrow closes), you should establish utilities service to the property. You will want to contact:

Phone company

Gas company

Electric company

Water company

Garbage collector

Post office

TIP

Don't worry about getting everything started too soon. It often takes the utilities a few weeks to get to the place. Give them the close-of-escrow date. If the close is delayed, call them and delay the turn-ons. It's far easier to get a utility to delay turning on the power than it is to get the utility to agree to come out there in the first place.

TIP

Be sure to write your name on the mailbox. Some postal employees will not deliver to a home unless the addressee's name is on the mailbox, even though the address on the letter may be correct! Also, be sure to fill out a "change of address" form at the post office.

TRAP

Be aware that many utility companies have been ripped off by people (usually tenants) who have established service and then after a few months have reneged on the bills. Thus, you may be required to put up a service deposit of as high as a $100 or more per utility. Try to avoid this cost whenever possible by "transferring" your service from your last residence instead of closing it out and opening new service at the new house.

Catch the In-Between Stuff

As soon as you move in, it's a good idea to check around the property to be sure that everything is as it should be. (You might not have noticed something in your final inspection, or something could have changed since then.) Here's a checklist when you buy a resale.

Checklist for Buying a Resale

	YES	NO
1. Is all fencing up and in place? (This is a particular concern if you have pets or small children.)	[ ]	[ ]
2. If you have a yard gate, does it close automatically? (A must if you have a pool.)	[ ]	[ ]
3. Do all the electrical switches, sockets, and appliances work?	[ ]	[ ]
4. Do you smell gas escaping anywhere, but particularly around heaters and stoves? (If yes, open all the windows and call the gas company immediately. Do not light any matches or try to find the leak yourself.)	[ ]	[ ]
5. Are there any water leaks at the water heater or elsewhere?	[ ]	[ ]
6. Is the paint and appearance of the exterior and interior as you expected it to be?	[ ]	[ ]
7. Are there any cracked windows or windows that don't function?	[ ]	[ ]

	YES	NO
8. Do all the doors close properly?	[ ]	[ ]
9. Has the previous owner left anything behind that should be returned?	[ ]	[ ]
10. Is there anything unusual or out of place that you might want to mention to someone?	[ ]	[ ]

All the above are usually relatively simple problems. By that, I mean that they're probably not worth getting upset about. There's bound to be some wear and tear on the property. It's to be expected, as are sticky windows and doors. After all, it's not a brand-new house.

If the previous owners left something behind, give them or their agent a call. If the water heater leaks, call up the warranty service (which you should have bought) or the seller's agent. Either one will most likely be happy to take care of it for you. The same holds true for safety problems such as a gate that doesn't close automatically or gas leaks.

TIP

I use this rule of thumb when buying a property. If the problems are going to cost $50 or less to fix, I take care of them myself. If they cost more than that, I complain to the seller or the seller's agent.

Remember, there are always going to be some problems when moving into a resale. If you expect them, they won't get out of hand.

Watch Out for the Big Stuff

And then there's the big stuff, problems which are major, serious, and need your special attention before they get out of hand. Here's a list of what to look for.

Checklist for the Big Stuff

	YES	NO
1. Does the seller (or seller's agent) refuse to handle any of the smaller stuff?	[ ]	[ ]

	YES	NO
2. Is there major damage?	[ ]	[ ]
3. Did the sellers lie about or omit something important regarding the property?	[ ]	[ ]
4. Is there a problem with the mortgage, the title, or the monies involved?	[ ]	[ ]
5. Is there anything else wrong which keeps you from sleeping at night?	[ ]	[ ]

If you answer yes to any of the above, then you've stepped out of the ordinary adjustment problems that any buyers face when moving in, and have entered the realm of big-time problems. Let's consider them one at a time.

1. *The sellers (or their agent) refuse to take care of any of the little things that have gone wrong.* My suggestion is that if the problems are little, still forget it. The hassle of fighting someone over half a dozen minor things isn't worth the upset stomach and potential heart attack you can get over it. I believe one of the best pieces of advice in the world is still, "Don't sweat the small stuff."

TRAP

On the other hand, add together enough small stuff and it can become pretty big. If the sellers won't listen to you, have your lawyer (the one you used on the deal) write them a letter. People respond surprisingly quickly to letters from attorneys. Even better, if the sellers' agent won't listen, write a letter of complaint to your state's real estate regulatory body. But before you send it to the state, send a copy to the agent with a note that says, "Do I really need to send this, or can we settle reasonably now?"

It's surprising how quickly agents respond when their license to practice real estate is threatened.

2. *Is there major damage?* What's major damage? Broken beams, cracked floors, ruined carpets, drapes, or paint? You'll know major when you see major.

Generally speaking, there are two kinds of major damage: disclosed and undisclosed. If the damage was disclosed to you before the sale was completed (usually in the form of a letter or form that you signed for having received), you're probably stuck with it. You knew about it and you still accepted the property. The sellers aren't going to be the least bit sympathetic and, chances are, neither is anyone else.

On the other hand, there's undisclosed damage. The worst case I ever saw was when sellers left on a vacation about 3 weeks prior to the close of escrow—with two cats locked inside their house.

The cats had adequate food and water, but were not trained to use a small box of kitty litter left for their benefit. In those 3 weeks they ruined the carpet. However, to see the carpet was not to know the problem, because upon returning home, the aghast sellers immediately had it cleaned. The problem was the odor, which could not be removed from the carpeting.

For the final walk-through, the sellers used air fresheners and opened all the windows, so the buyers had no idea there was a problem.

It became quite evident to the buyers what the problem was, however, the first night they moved in. When it got cold in the evening, they closed the windows and went to sleep. The odor welled up, causing allergic reactions in the children and forcing the buyers to move to a motel.

What could the buyers do?

They demanded that the sellers correct the problem. That is, they demanded all new wall-to-wall carpeting throughout the house—at a cost of over $12,000!

The sellers, at first, refused to pay—until it became evident to them that the problem did exist and that they had not disclosed it. Then their attorney suggested that they pay and move on, which they did.

3. *Did the sellers lie about or omit something important regarding the property?* Did they say the house was 10 years old and you flip over the top of the toilet bowl tank and see that it's 25 years old? (The date of manufacture of toilet bowl tanks is almost always inside the lid. Since these are rarely replaced, it often gives a good indication to the age of the property. Recorded building permits will give the official building date.) Did they forget to mention that there was toxic waste in the drainage canal behind the house? Did you discover on the third day that a previous tenant had been shot to death in the very bedroom in which you are now trying to sleep?

These sound like very severe problems, and any one of them might be cause for you to demand that the sellers repay you your money and take the house back. See your attorney at once.

4. *Is there a problem with the title or the mortgage?* Title problems are rare. If you have one, however, hang onto that policy of title insurance you bought. It's your guarantee that you'll get either clear title or your money back.

TIP

Call the title company at once if there's a problem. If the company refuses to fix it to your satisfaction, call the state real estate department or the appropriate agency in your state which governs title companies. It will investigate the problem for you.

The biggest problem with mortgage companies is that they sometimes get your loan payback account mixed up with someone else's. You owe $512 a month, but your new payment book comes in and it says you owe $3200 a month!

Don't get excited. Stay calm. Call the mortgage company to straighten it out.

TIP

Don't expect that the first person you talk to at the mortgage company will solve your problem. You may have to persist through several levels of management before you find someone in authority who can handle the problem. Eventually, however, it will get straightened out. The lender will insist on getting paid every penny owed. But the lender shouldn't take a penny more than is owed. (Otherwise, the lender could face enormous penalties.)

On the other hand, don't do the lender any favors.

One couple recently bought a home, obtaining a new adjustable-rate mortgage. The mortgage was supposed to be adjusted every 3 months. At the end of the fourth month, the buyers noticed that the lender hadn't made an adjustment, even though interest rates had gone up. At the end of the fifth month, still no change had been made. Wanting to do the right thing, the sellers wrote to the lender, explaining that the payments were too small.

Instead of thanking them, the lender immediately raised the payments, said the borrowers were delinquent in their fourth and fifth months (because they had paid too little), and put the property into foreclosure!

Yes, the problem eventually all got straightened out, but not before the lender insisted on and got an increase in those 2 months plus late penalties! I agree, it's a sad, but true, tale.

On the other hand, if the buyers had never bothered to tell the lender of its mistake...? A close reading of their loan documents revealed that once the adjustment period had passed, the lender would have had no further recourse. If the borrowers hadn't said anything and another 3 months had gone by (the adjustment period), the lender would have had to bear the responsibility of its own incompetence.

5. *If you can't sleep at night, you've got a problem.* The sooner you get it resolved, the sooner you'll get your sleep. Here are some alternatives:

Your Courses of Action When There Is a Serious Problem

1. Decide whether or not you can live with it.
2. If you can't live with it, call your agent and see if she or he can correct the problem.
3. If you get no satisfaction, call the sellers and their agent and demand a correction of the problem.
4. If you get no satisfaction, consider writing the state real estate licensing agency, but let the agent know first that you're planning to do so.
5. Call your attorney.

Index

About the Author

Robert Irwin has been a successful real estate broker for more than 30 years, helping buyers and sellers alike through every kind of real estate transaction. He also serves as a consultant to lender, investor, and brokers. Irwin is one of the most knowledgeable and prolific writers in the real estate field, with such books to his credit as *Tips & Traps When Selling a Home*; *Tips & Traps When Mortgage Hunting*; *Tips & Traps for Making Money in Real Estate*; *Tips & Traps for Saving on All Your Real Estate Taxes*; *Buy, Rent & Hold; How to Find Hidden Real Estate Bargains;* and *The McGraw-Hill Real Estate Handbook.* Robert Irwin is based in Los Angeles, California.